EASY
fresco

Lina Ferrara

STERLING

New York / London
www.sterlingpublishing.com

Prolific Impressions Production Staff:

Editor in Chief: Mickey Baskett
Copy Editor: Ellen Glass
Graphics: Dianne Miller, Karen Turpin
Styling: Lenos Key
Photography: Jerry Mucklow
Administration: Jim Baskett

Every effort has been made to insure that the information presented is accurate. Since we have no control over physical conditions, individual skills, or chosen tools and products, the publisher disclaims any liability for injuries, losses, untoward results, or any other damages which may result from the use of the information in this book. Thoroughly read the instructions for all products used to complete the projects in this book, paying particular attention to all cautions and warnings shown for that product to ensure their proper and safe use.

Library of Congress Cataloging-in-Publication Data

Ferrara, Lina.
 Easy fresco / Lina Ferrara.
   p. cm.
 Includes index.
 ISBN-13: 978-1-4027-3157-0
1. Texture painting--Amateurs' manuals. 2. Furniture painting--Amateurs' manuals. 3. House painting--Amateurs' manuals. 4. Handicraft. I. Title.

TT323.F47 2008
745.7'23--dc22

                                    2007052569
10 9 8 7 6 5 4 3 2 1

Published by Sterling Publishing Co., Inc.
387 Park Avenue South, New York, NY 10016
© 2008 by Prolific Impressions, Inc.
Distributed in Canada by Sterling Publishing
c/o Canadian Manda Group, 165 Dufferin Street
Toronto, Ontario, Canada M6K 3H6
Distributed in the United Kingdom by GMC Distribution Services
Castle Place, 166 High Street, Lewes, East Sussex, England BN7 1XU
Distributed in Australia by Capricorn Link (Australia) Pty. Ltd.
P.O. Box 704, Windsor, NSW 2756, Australia

Sterling ISBN 978-1-4027-3157-0

For information about custom editions, special sales, premium and corporate purchases, please contact Sterling Special Sales Department at 800-805-5489 or specialsales@sterlingpublishing.com.

About the Artist

LINA FERRARA has been teaching and demonstrating fine art and decorative painting for more than 20 years. She has traveled extensively across the United States and in Europe, presenting workshops in Canada, Holland, and Italy, and studying gilding and traditional Italian decorative painting in Florence, Italy. She currently resides in rural central Pennsylvania, where she draws her inspiration for vibrant representational artwork of still life, flowers, landscapes, and animals.

Lina enjoys working in all media including oil, acrylic, watercolor, and graphite while exploring both traditional and nontraditional surfaces ranging from canvas, paper, and wood to glass and tile. Her award-winning work can be found in private collections in the United States, Italy, Holland, and Germany.

"I love painting luminous objects, especially grapes and pottery. Both fruit and handmade pottery have an organic quality that I want to capture on canvas. I also love the decorative painting of Italy with its rich and varied forms. Most of my work features traditional subject matter, but I don't like to limit myself to one genre or medium."

Teaching and demonstrating nationally since 1992 at conferences and trade shows and for art associations, Lina provides her students with extensive technical knowledge, while instilling in them the confidence they need to pursue subjects of their own interest. Lina feels that mastering basic technique is key to developing individual style. **You can see her work at www.linaferrara.com.**

ACKNOWLEDGEMENTS

I'd like to express my appreciation to the companies whose products were used in the creation of the projects in this book.

- *For Texture products and tools, and Americana Paint:* DecoArt, Inc., P.O. Box 386, Stanford, KY 40484, www.decoart.com
- *For Opulence gel medium, Wood Texture/Filler, and Pure Color colorants:* TerraBella Finishes, P.O. Box 940718, Simi Valley, CA 93094, www.terrabellafinishes.com
- *For Omni-Gel medium:* Houston Art, Inc., 10770 Moss Ridge Road, Houston, TX 77043, www.houstonart.com
- *For stencils:* Rebecca Baer, Inc., 13316 Marsh Pike, Hagerstown, MD 21742, www.rebeccabaer.com
- *For stamps and stencils:* Delta Technical Coatings, Inc., 2550 Pellissier Place, Whittier, CA 90601, www.deltacrafts.com
- *For Fabri-Tac and Quick Grip glues:* Beacon Adhesives, Inc., 125 MacQuesten Parkway South, Mount Vernon, NY 10550, www.beaconadhesives.com
- *For stencil cutter and wooden plate:* Walnut Hollow, 1409 State Road 23, Dodgeville, WI 53533, www.walnuthollow.com
- *For metallic wax:* J.W. Etc., 1212 N. Tancahua Street, Corpus Christi, TX 78401, www.jwetc.com
- *For texturing tools, FolkArt® acrylic paint, FolkArt® Crackle Medium, Mod Podge Glue/Finish for Decoupage, Stencil Decor® stencils:* Plaid Enterprises, Inc., Norcross, GA 30091, www.plaidonline.com

A Special Thanks

to **Rose Wilde** of The Wood Icing Company for contributing beautifully designed furniture projects created with Wood Icing Textura Paste and Fissure Size, a crackling medium. The Wood Icing Company, P.O. Box 8, Foristell, MO 63348, 1-866-966-3423, www.woodicing.com

TABLE OF CONTENTS

INTRODUCTION

I have loved the feeling of old world textures and finishes from my childhood. I can remember the old stone and stucco walls of my grandfather's farmhouse in southern Italy. The uneven textures and mottled colors still appeal to me and the natural, organic quality is one I tried to recreate for you. Using the mediums available today makes creating textured finishes so much fun and so easy.

You can apply texture mediums to all types of surfaces, both new and old. Anything from small boxes to large furniture pieces to cabinet doors and walls can be transformed with texture products and the paint treatments in this book. You can even rescue items that would otherwise be discarded.

Some of the projects presented here have a traditional feeling and use images from Old Master painters in the form of posters and prints. Some have a more modern twist, using embedded objects and trendy colors. Experiment and create something you will be proud to display in your home.

My joy would be that the techniques presented here inspire you to create other projects. Use these ideas as a springboard to your own creative works. Everyone has the capacity for creating beautiful works of art. Don't be afraid to take that first step, get paint on your hands, and listen to your own voice of inspiration.

Photos by Chris Little Photography.

*Pictured above: These stunning wall niches combine texture with decoupaged art prints. This special technique was created by custom finisher, Kass Wilson. See Kass's book, **Creative Finishes** published by Sterling Publishing Co.*

Pictured left: A closeup of this beautiful wall niche.

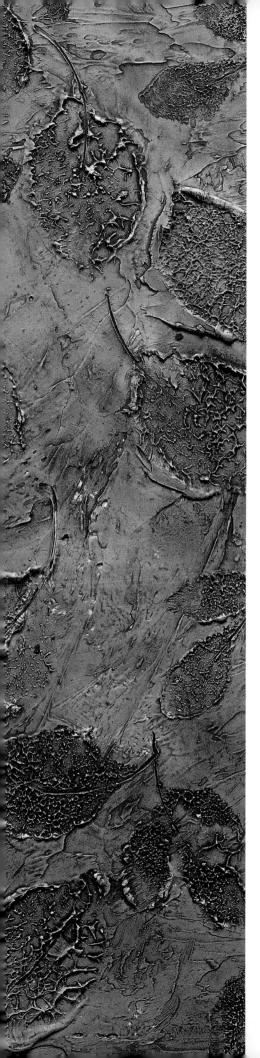

CHAPTER 1

General Supplies

You can create these warm, textured finishes that are shown on furniture, boxes, and other small objects using modern materials and techniques that have been developed with today's crafters in mind. Texturing supplies are easy to find at local craft shops or do-it-yourself shops and are easy to work with.

A work of art is above all an adventure of the mind.
Eugene Ionesco

TEXTURE PRODUCTS

Texture mediums come in different thicknesses and all have different properties. Some have more body; some can be crumbly. The only way to really see which one will give you the effect you like is to experiment with several products on demo boards made from sturdy illustration board, foam core, or canvas board. You will soon settle on your own favorite.

Some products are colored, some white, and some clear. You can add color to most of the products with acrylic paint or colorants. Depending on how much coloring product you add, it may thin the consistency of the texture product, can affect the thickness, and may alter the drying time.

Dried texture mediums are usually not flexible. If the surface that you put it on is subject to bending, the product may crack or flake off.

Textures Available:

THICK TEXTURE

- **Venetian plaster**, also called polished plaster or Italian plaster, dries to a very hard, durable finish that can be burnished to a marble-like sheen. Available where do-it-yourself products are sold.

- **Paper texture** gives a rocky texture that absorbs paint in the same manner as watercolor paper. Apply with a palette knife and pat the product on. Available where craft supplies are sold.

- **Thick texture:** Large particles give the product a grainy texture.

- **Crackle texture** dries crumbly, like old plaster. Use any of the application techniques. (It is different from "crackle medium," which is a product that is explained later.)

- **Wood texture** is smooth with a few particles. It lends itself to any kind of application.

MEDIUM TEXTURE

- **Modeling paste** is very smooth and thinner than some of the other products. It has versatile applications.

- **Clear medium (decoupage medium, clear dimensional medium, or glass texture):** Products with a thinner consistency that dry clear. They can be used with any application techniques in instances where you want to see what is underneath. They give a smooth, shiny finish.

- **Texture paste** is a latex based product with the consistency of peanut butter. It maintains details from stencils and stamps. When dried and stained, it creates a carved wood appearance.

- **Stucco** comes in many colors and gives a smooth texture that works well with any of the application methods.

- **Drywall compound** can be used in place of some of the other texture products. It gives a smooth finish, but is prone to cracking and flaking if the surface is flexed.

FINE TEXTURE

• **Sand texture** is grainy and appears almost like concrete when dry.

• **Fine texture** contains very fine particles and can be used with any of the application techniques.

Pictured right: Untinted Venetian plaster.

EXAMPLES OF TEXTURES

Thick

Crackle

Wood

Paper Texture

Stucco

Modeling Paste

Clear

Sand Texture

Fine Texture

CRACKLE PRODUCTS

Crackle products give added texture to your projects. Antiquing settles in the cracks and crevices, making them darker than the surface and enhancing the dimensional qualities of the texture.

TWO TYPES OF CRACKLE MEDIUMS

There are two types of crackle products. In one, the surface is painted with acrylic or latex paint and allowed to dry. The crackle medium is applied over the basecoated surface. When the crackle medium is dry, a layer of a contrasting color of paint is applied on top of it. The top layer of paint cracks as it dries, revealing bits of the base color. This type of crackle medium is used in many of the projects in this book.

The second type of crackle is applied to the finished surface. It will dry clear, cracking as it dries. The cracks are revealed during the antiquing process.

*Crackled texture gives an aged fresco appearance to this decoupaged print. See the "Floral Frescoes" project in **Chapter 3: Decoupage Frescoes** for instructions.*

COLORING & ANTIQUING AGENTS

You can add color to texture medium products before application or after the texture medium has dried. Keep a record of the kind and quantity of coloring agents you used in case you want to mix the same color again. Apply the colored product to a sample board and write the recipe on the back of the board.

Antiquing the textured and crackled surface adds depth and an old world patina to the look. You can purchase pre-mixed antiquing or use acrylic paint mixed into a glazing medium.

ACRYLIC PAINTS

Acrylic paint can be mixed into the texture medium to color it, brushed onto the textured surface or the surface of the project, or used to antique the textured surface. It can be used on almost all types of surfaces and dries to a matte finish. Acrylic paints can also be mixed into a glazing medium to create an antiquing.

- Premixed **craft paints** can be applied right out of the bottle. Just squeeze out the amount you want and begin painting.
- When clarity of color is important, such as in the antiquing process, use **artist quality bottled paints or artist's tube acrylics**. These are highly pigmented paints and can be mixed to create an unlimited spectrum of colors.

Acrylic paints clean up easily with soap and water.

Coloring agents

UNIVERSAL TINTS

Liquid pigments known as *universal tints* are available in art supply stores, paint stores, and home improvement stores. They can be used to color waterbased or oil-based paints or stains and to color texture medium.

Add the tint a few drops at a time, stirring well, until you achieve the color you want. For a consistent appearance, you must mix thoroughly to blend the pigments into the product. Follow a color formula or simply mix colors you like.

OIL COLORS

You can use oil based products to create antiqued finishes. They dry slowly, giving you a longer open time than acrylics. Do not mix oil paints into texture medium. If you antique with oil paints, use an oil or solvent-based varnish.

MICA POWDERS

Add iridescent color to your texture projects with mica powders made from finely ground minerals. Stir the powders into the texture product before you apply texture to your surface; mix thoroughly for a consistent appearance. You can find mica powders at art supply stores and paint stores.

PAINT ADDITIVES

You can mix extenders into water-based paints and mediums to slow the drying time and to increase the open time for blending colors. The paint can be dried with a hairdryer if you are in a hurry.

GLAZING MEDIUM

To create layers of color and high-lights, or to antique the item and emphasize the texture, mix clear, **waterbased glazing medium** with acrylic paint and apply it over the dried texture. Clear glazing medium is a transparent gel or liquid sold in art supply stores; it comes in jars, bottles, or cans. Keep precise notes when you add color to the glazing medium so you can mix more if you run out before you finish your project.

Pre-tinted **antiquing glazes** are convenient for antiquing. If you run out, simply buy more of the same color.

TEXTURING TOOLS

Texturing tools are easy to find and can be as close as your kitchen or garage. Some of the tools you can use are:

METAL BLADES

Metal blades, such as a palette knife, putty knife, or trowel can be used to spread and texture the texturing medium. Metal blades are more durable than plastic blades. Tools are available in various widths; use a blade that fits the size of the area you are filling with texture product.

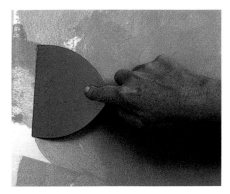

SPECIALTY TEXTURING TOOLS

There are many tools available that give a variety of textures. Some examples are texturing combs, mitts, grainers. You can find these where faux finishing products are sold.

PLASTIC UTENSILS

Plastic utensils, such as a spatula, spoon, fork, or knife are convenient because they are inexpensive, are disposable, are easy to use, and create interesting textures.

PAINT ROLLERS

You can use paint rollers to apply texture products. A roller cover with a 3/8" nap is a good choice. Use a lower quality, less expensive roller to apply plaster; use a better quality roller to apply glazes. You can also use dense foam rollers to apply texture products. Choose rollers that are suitable for the size of your project.

SPONGES

Sponges, both kitchen sponges and natural sea sponges are used to add texture to products with a thin consistency. They are great to use for texturizing, or applying antiquing and colored glazes.

BRUSHES

UTILITY BRUSHES

- **Foam brushes**: Use these disposable brushes for basecoating, applying antiquing, or applying decoupage medium or glue. Use only on smooth surfaces. A foam brush may tear on the rough surface of dried texture, and leave little pieces of debris in the paint or finish.
- **Chip brushes** are inexpensive flat paintbrushes that can be used for antiquing as well as applying paint or glue. Keep various sizes on hand, and use the size that fits the area of your design.

ARTIST'S BRUSHES

Use high quality artist's brushes when detail is important, and to create some dry brush effects and textured brushstrokes. With flowing media like watercolor and acrylic, a brush is valued for its spring (the ability of the brush to return to its original shape), absorbency, point, and edge durability. Artist's brushes come in many sizes. Recommended brushes for the projects in this book:

- Round – #6, for decorative painting and finishing details
- Flat – 1", for decorative painting and basecoating small areas
- Liner, for decorative painting and outlining
- Fan brush, for dry brush antiquing effects
- Filbert – #8, for decorative painting and creating brushstroke texture

BRUSH CARE

Good brushes are an investment that will last a long time with proper care.

- When loading, using or cleaning, work the hairs in their natural direction.
- Do not leave a brush soaking in liquid for extended periods of time.
- Never leave a brush resting on its bristles.
- Take care never to let paint work up into the ferrule.
- Never allow paint to dry in the brush.

Cleaning Your Brushes

- Rinse your brushes as you work, and clean your brushes promptly when you finish working.
- Press the bristles gently across a bar of mild soap. Rinse and repeat as often as necessary until no paint color shows on the soap.
- Allow brushes to lie flat on a paper towel while drying.
- Store brushes lying flat or with heads upright so there is no pressure on the hair.

OTHER SUPPLIES

SURFACES

You can decorate any type of surface from metal to wood, old or new There are a multitude of possibilities and sources of surfaces.

- Furniture – old or new unfinished
- Metal decorative accessories
- Cabinet doors
- Canvas – mounted or unmounted
- Wooden trays, plaques, and boxes
- Paper mache items
- Garage sale finds
- Photograph albums
- Plates
- Frames and mirrors

VARNISH

Apply a layer of protection to your finished piece. Polyurethane varnishes are suitable for using over texture products. Varnishes come in three degrees of gloss — matte (the least shiny), satin, or gloss (very shiny and slick).

When working with waterbased paints and products, finish with a waterbased varnish. When working with oil-based stains, paints, and products, finish with an oil-based or solvent-based varnish.

OTHER PRODUCTS

Glue is used for general crafting techniques such as gluing on trims.

Cloth rags, for wiping antiquing mixtures. They can be purchased at paint stores and hardware stores. You can also use **shop towels**, which are heavy duty paper towels that resist breaking down when wet.

Stirring sticks in several sizes, for mixing colorants into textures and stirring paints and varnishes.

Palette, plastic foam plates, or clean deli packaging trays, for holding paints and antiquing mixtures.

Water containers, one for rinsing brushes and one for clean water to thin paint or medium. You can use an artist's water basin or plastic margarine tubs.

Sandpaper, in various grades, for preparing surfaces and smoothing dried texture.

Tack cloth, for removing sanding dust.

Painter's tape, to mask off trim areas and to secure stencils and patterns to surfaces. Use a low tack, high quality tape that is less likely to pull up bits of texture.

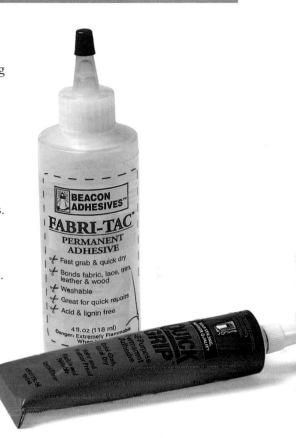

Paper towels, for wiping tools and general cleanup.

Dishpan filled with water, for holding tools until you can clean them. There is often no time to wash tools while you are working with fast-drying texture mediums. To keep the mediums from drying on and ruining tools, stencils, and stamps, toss them into clean water until you are finished and can take the time to wash them in soapy water.

Plastic tablecloth, drop cloth, or pieces of cardboard for protecting your work area.

CHAPTER 2

Creating Textures

It is easy to add texture to almost any surface—walls, wood furniture pieces, canvas, pressed board and more. You can achieve different effects by using different texture products-smooth and thin or grainy and thick-and a variety of tools.

In this chapter you will learn the basics: how to prepare your surface, how to apply the texture medium, how to antique it to bring out its surface qualities, and how to finish it. Later chapters will cover special effects for combining texture with decoupage, stenciling, and embossing to create a true fresco look.

PREPARING THE SURFACE

You can decorate any surface with texture-old or new metal, wood, ceramic, or textile. Buy new pieces or have fun searching for older items at garage sales, flea markets, and antique stores. It is not always necessary to strip and sand old furniture. The texture completely covers chipped paint and missing veneer.

Work outdoors or in a well-ventilated area. Wear chemical resistant gloves, eye protection, and long pants and a long-sleeved shirt when using chemicals and harsh or toxic cleaners. Follow the instructions on the product labels. You may wish to wear a mask when sanding.

NEW WOOD

1. Clean the surface if necessary. Remove dust or particles with a tack cloth.
2. Fill any holes with wood filler.
3. Sand wood with the grain. Use medium grit (100) sandpaper if the wood feels rough. If it feels smooth use fine grit (220) sandpaper. Remove sanding dust with a tack cloth or a damp cloth.
4. Seal with wood sealer. Be sure to seal all surfaces; unsealed areas can absorb or lose moisture and cause warping or cracking of the wood.
5. Sand lightly again, to smooth the grain of the wood that was raised by the sealer. Remove sanding dust with a tack cloth or a damp cloth.

OLD WOOD

1. Scrape off peeling or flaking paint.
2. Using #0000 steel wool and denatured alcohol, rub the surface to loosen dirt and old finish. It may take several applications to remove the old finish. You may choose to clean dirty pieces with a prepared furniture cleaner or a heavy duty cleaner that contains trisodium phosphate (TSP) sold at paint and hardware stores.
3. Sand wood with the grain.
4. Allow the surface to dry completely before basecoating.

METAL

1. Clean the surface if necessary. Remove dust or particles with a tack cloth.
2. If there are any rust spots, treat the metal with a rust-inhibiting coating containing phosphoric acid, or with naval jelly. Either product will remove rust and help to prevent the rust from returning.
3. Remove any traces of dirt or oil by scrubbing the surface with non-abrasive or mildly abrasive cleanser. Rinse with clear water. Another method is to rinse with diluted vinegar solution—1 part vinegar to 1 part water.
4. Sand lightly with 180-220 grit sandpaper. This will provide tooth and help the sealer to adhere to the metal.
5. Seal with one coat of multipurpose sealer. If you wish, you can add background color to the sealer at a 1:1 ratio. To avoid ridges, apply several thin coats of sealer instead of one thick coat, and brush out well. Apply additional coats of background color until you achieve the desired coverage.

BASECOATING

The surface can be painted either before or after the texture is added. When painting an overall color after texture has been added to the surface:
1. Thin the paint with water so as not to fill in the texture with heavy areas of paint.
2. Use a chip brush or an old artist's brush to base-coat. A foam brush may tear on the rough surface and leave little pieces of sponge in the paint.

APPLYING TEXTURE MEDIUM

The texture medium can be left white and painted after drying, or it can be tinted before it is applied. Some texture products can be purchased already tinted.

When you mix a batch of colored texture medium, keep a record of the colors, amounts, and kind of colorant you use. You may need to mix the same texture color again. To achieve a consistent appearance, mix thoroughly, using a wooden stir stick or an electric drill with a mixer attachment.

TINTING TEXTURE MEDIUM

Texture medium may be tinted by adding:
- Acrylic paints: Artist tube acrylics, artist quality bottled acrylics, or premixed craft acrylics.
- Universal tints: Liquid pigments. Add a few drops at a time and mix well until you achieve the color you want.
- Mica powders: Iridescent color made from ground minerals.

(Refer to "Coloring Agents" in the "General Supplies" section for more information.)

APPLYING TEXTURE MEDIUM

A metal blade or palette knife is best for this task. Depending upon how much medium you are using and the size of your tools, the medium might be easier to work with if it were scooped onto a disposable foam plate or a paint tray.

Tinting plaster by adding drops of universal tints.

Photo 1. *Scoop the texture medium from the container or tray with a metal blade or palette knife.*

Photo 2. *Place the medium onto the surface.*

Photo 3. *Spread the texture medium, keeping a random motion so as not to set up a pattern. Hold the blade at a 30 degree angle to the surface as you spread. Various tools can be used to give the medium additional texture.*

USING TOOLS TO CREATE TEXTURE

Tools can be as simple as utensils you have on hand in the kitchen or garage, or you can use specialized tools from the home improvement store or art supply store. Practicing on sample boards will help you decide what product and texturing technique will give you the best effect for the surface you have chosen to decorate. Sample boards can be stiff cardboard, canvas board, foam core, or plywood. Write on the board the products and techniques you used. Experiment with different tools and try the prepackaged specialty tools. Keep in mind that antiquing the finished piece will enhance the details.

Choose tools suitable to the size of the surface you want to cover. If you are working on a wall or a piece of furniture, use larger tools. If you are working on smaller items such as boxes or canvas wall pieces, create more delicate textures by using smaller proportioned tools.

USING A METAL BLADE

Example 1

1. Scoop the texture medium from the container with a blade and smooth the medium on the surface.
2. While the texture medium is still wet, use the blade to give texture. Skim over the top of the product; this will give a more fractured appearance to the surface. *(Photo 4)* Using the knife to drag deeply will give a different appearance.

Photo 4

Example 2

A thicker layer of texture medium makes higher peaks. Use less medium to achieve a more refined look. Vary the thickness of the medium to achieve more variation in the texture.

1. Scoop the texture medium from the container with a blade and smooth the medium on the surface.
2. Hold the palette knife flat on the surface, then lift the knife straight up, leaving peaks of texture. Continue the up and down movement of the knife to texture the rest of the surface.

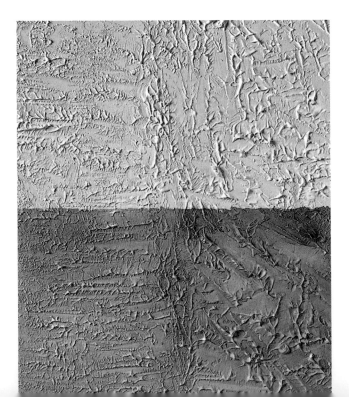

USING A SPONGE

Example 3

1. Scoop the texture medium from the container with a metal blade and smooth it over the surface.
2. While the medium is wet, dab the surface with a sponge in an up and down movement. This will give an even, overall texture. *(Photo 5)*

Photo 5

USING PLASTIC WRAP

Example 4

The plastic wrap gives a great variation in effect, leaving little craters in the surface that are hard to get with other techniques.

1. Scoop the texture medium from the container with a palette knife and smooth it over the surface. Smooth the medium a bit more.
2. Place a sheet of plastic wrap on the surface. Press it down with your hands. *(Photo 6)*
3. Lift off the plastic wrap and discard it. *(Photo 7)*

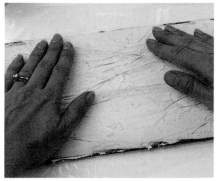

Photo 6

Photo 7

Using Tools to Create Texture
Continued from page 23

USING A COMBING TOOL OR FORK

Example 5: Combing Tool

1. Apply the texture medium to the surface and smooth it to an even layer with a palette knife.
2. Holding the combing tool at a 90-degree angle to the surface, drag through the texture medium, straight across the board. *(Photo 8)* Clean off the tool after every pass.
3. Make parallel strokes with the tool in one direction, or cross strokes for a basket-weave effect. *(Photo 9)*

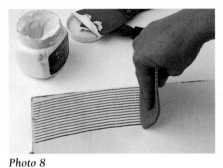

Photo 8   Photo 9

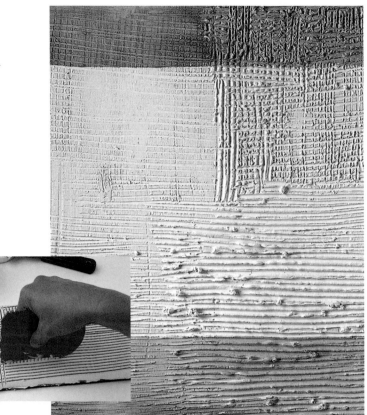

Example 6: Fork

1. Apply the texture medium to the surface and smooth it to an even layer with a palette knife.
2. Create circles or swirls with the fork. *(Photo 10)* Wipe the fork often on a paper towel.
3. Try other patterns or combine different patterns. If you don't like the effect, just smooth over the texture with the palette knife and try something else.

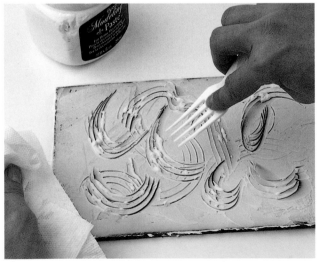

Photo 10

USING A SPOON

Example 7

1. Apply the texture medium to the surface and smooth it to an even layer with a palette knife.

2. Use the spoon to make depressions in the texture in an allover, uniform pattern. This technique leaves a rougher texture reminiscent of old exterior plaster walls.

Photo 10

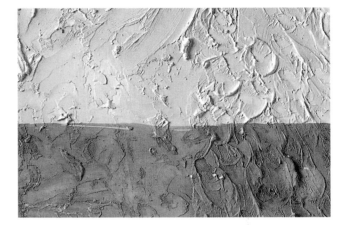

CREATING A CRACKLED FINISH

You can create cracks in the texture with several methods. Antiquing the finished project will emphasize the cracks.

1. **Texture crackle product:** Use a texture product that is specially formulated to crack as it dries.

2. **Thick coat:** (This is not as reliable as the other methods.) Apply the texture medium in a very thick coat. Dry with a hairdryer. This will dry the very top surface first, leaving the layer underneath still wet, causing cracks to appear.

3. **Crackle medium:** Apply crackle medium to a painted surface or on top of the dried texture. Add a topcoat of varnish or the topcoat specified for use with the crackle medium. The crackle medium will be sandwiched between the two finishes. Cracks will appear as the product dries. Follow the manufacturer's instructions.

Crackle medium was used to create the cracked texture on this canvas. See the "Pieta Canvas" project (in Chapter 3: Decoupage Frescoes) for complete instructions.

ANTIQUING METHODS

Antiquing your textured surface will show off its dimensional effects and nuances. Make sure that the texture is thoroughly dried and cured before rubbing the antiquing as some of the texture may flake off, especially if it is heavily applied. Some texture products tend to flake more than others.

The surface can be antiqued heavily, leaving much of the color on the surface, or lightly, depending on your preference. The antiquing on the Autumn Vineyard Tray (in *Chapter 3: Decoupage Frescoes*) has a heavier, more substantial feel than the lighter, more airy antiquing on the Painted Roses in the Round project (in *Chapter 6: Additional Fun & Easy Techniques*).

ANTIQUING WITH ACRYLIC PAINTS

Thin acrylic paint with extender medium or a glazing medium for a transparent or translucent color that will settle into the cracks and crevices and still allow what is underneath to show through. Remove excess color with a soft, lint free cloth or a paper towel. (Use a shop towel or other sturdy paper towel that will not disintegrate and leave fuzzy pieces in the antiquing.) Allow some darker color to remain on the edges and corners of the surface.

Color Suggestions
- Burnt Umber
- Raw Umber
- Ultramarine Blue + Black
- Match one of the dark colors on the surface if you are antiquing over a print.

Acrylic Paint Thinned with Water
Use for small projects or where a smooth color transition is not necessary.
1. Thin acrylic paint with water to the consistency of ink. Mix a quantity sufficient to antique the entire project.
2. Apply with a soft brush or a natural sponge.
3. Wipe back with a cloth or paper towel.

Acrylic Paint Thinned with a Extender Medium
Extender gives you more time to manipulate the color. For a lighter antiquing effect, apply a thin coat of the medium to the surface and begin the antiquing process while it is wet.
1. Thin acrylic paint with medium to the consistency of ink. Mix a quantity sufficient to antique the entire project.
2. Apply with a soft brush or a natural sponge.
3. Wipe back with a cloth or paper towel.
4. With a dry artist's mop brush, lightly dust the surface of the painting to soften the brushstrokes. Where you want greater color dispersion, tap the mop brush up and down on the area, wipe off the excess paint from the brush with a paper towel, and dust the brush softly over the surface.

Note: When using a medium it is important not to dampen the cloth, paper towel, or brush with water, because it will remove the color and cause splotchy areas.

Photo 12. Mix paint with extender or glazing medium to an inky consistency.

Photo 13. Apply with a foam brush or a chip brush.

Photo 14. Wipe the antiquing from the surface with a soft cloth.

Photo 15. Lightly dust the surface with a mop brush to soften the antiquing.

ANTIQUING WITH TINTED GLAZING MEDIUM

Glazing medium is a gel or liquid that is sold in art supply stores, packaged in bottles, cans, or tubs. Apply it and wipe it back just as you would water-thinned antiquing mix. Tint clear, waterbased glazing medium with universal tints or acrylic paints. Keep careful notes about the amounts and colorants you use, so you can mix more if you run out.

- **Mix with universal tints:** Add tints drop by drop, mixing thoroughly. Makes a transparent glaze.
- **Mix with acrylic paints:** Tint with bottled craft acrylic paints. Makes a less transparent glaze than universal tints.
- **Premixed antiquing products:** Convenient if you can find the color you want. You can buy more of the same color if needed.

ANTIQUING WITH MULTIPLE COLORS

Add additional colors while the first layer of color is still wet; the colors will blend to create additional colors. As an alternative, antique with one color and let dry; re-wet the surface with extender, then antique with additional colors.

Continued on next page

Antiquing Methods
Continued from page 27

ENHANCING ANTIQUING

Remove some of the antiquing color by wiping while it is still wet to reveal the peaks of the texture, or it can be removed when the antiquing has dried. The effect is slightly different, but both methods enhance the surface interest by leaving deeper color in the wrinkles, tiny pits, and crevices of the texture.

Dry Brushing (top of photo): Let the surface dry. Load a stiff brush (an artist's fan brush is recommended) with a light color of acrylic paint. Wipe most of the paint off on a dry paper towel. Using a light touch, gently rake the brush across the surface, hitting just the peaks of the texture. Resist the urge to press harder as you run out of paint. Reload the dry brush, wipe on the paper towel, and continue.

Buffing (bottom of photo): Let the surface dry. Buff with a dry cloth or paper towel. Even more color may be removed if desired with a paper towel moistened with water.

FINISHING

VARNISHING

Varnish the surface to protect it from dust, dirt, and fingerprints and make it easier to clean. The texture, paint, and antiquing must be completely dry before you varnish.

Varnishes come in three degrees of gloss: matte (the least shiny), satin, or gloss (very shiny and slick). To determine the level of gloss that looks best on your project, brush water on the surface. If you prefer that look to the way the surface looks when it is dry, use a satin or gloss varnish. Projects that have metallic embellishments usually require a satin or gloss finish.

- Apply varnish with a large, soft brush to avoid brush marks.
- Varnish the most important surface first.
- Place the fully loaded brush in the center of the surface and work out. A fully loaded brush on the edge creates drips.
- Avoid bubbles by going slowly and brushing in one direction.

- Most varnish products are self leveling, so they will dry to a clear, even surface. If you speed dry with a hairdryer, the varnish does not have time to level.
- Apply several thin coats rather than one thick coat. Dry after each coat.

WAX

Some waxes add a yellowish color to the project, giving the effect of greater age to the antiqued surface. There are also specific antiquing waxes that can be used to age the surface further or add a metallic sheen. Some brands of floor wax or fine furniture wax are clear and do not add additional color to your piece.

- Apply wax either after varnishing or as a protective coat by itself.
- Rub on the wax with a soft cloth. Use circular motions and cover the entire surface.
- Buff with a clean, soft cloth. Do not wait for the wax to dry because it is then too difficult to remove from the texture.

CHAPTER 3

Decoupage Frescoes

Give prints and posters extra visual impact with texture and antiquing. The decorative results are worth the effort, and your home will proudly display one-of-a-kind examples of your creative work. The mellow colors and classical themes of Old Master paintings are particularly well suited to the antiqued fresco treatment. Prints and posters are easy to find at museum shops and in catalogs. Another good source of images is wallpaper borders; they come in colors and designs that complement contemporary home decor trends.

When you combine a design print with texture medium in this technique, the print appears to be part of the texture. The print is usually adhered to the painted surface first, before any texture medium is applied. The decoupage and aging effects marry the print with the texture.

SUPPLIES

CHOOSING PAPERS

Almost anything on paper can be used as long as it can be wet without the ink or color running. Test a small section with water. Some suitable materials are:
• Prints, new or old
• Posters
• Clippings from magazines, catalogs, or old books
• Postcards or greeting cards, new or old
• Wallpaper borders or sections, including textured wallpapers
• Decorative papers including handmade papers, scrapbook papers, tissue papers, and papers made especially for decoupage
• Wrapping paper
• Fabric swatches

Using Prints: The print should look as if it is *part of* the texture or as if it is *under* the texture. Usually you will glue the print to the painted surface first, then add texture medium and antiquing on top of the print. If the print is on very thin paper, it can be adhered on top of the textured surface.
Thinner papers show the underlying texture better; however, they are more fragile. Thin the decoupage medium with water before applying it to the surface.
Thicker papers will stand more manipulation and can even be moved or repositioned while the decoupage medium is still wet. Apply decoupage medium to both the back of the paper and the surface. It is a bit more difficult to work out the air bubbles, so carefully press the paper to the surface and smooth down with a brayer.

When choosing images, try to use papers of the same thickness on any one project.

DECOUPAGE MEDIUM

A variety of glues and mediums can be used for decoupage; you can even use thinned white craft glue. The best choice is an artist's medium type of decoupage product that is archival and dries clear, not milky. Read the label for product information.

BRAYER AND WALLPAPER SEAM ROLLER

A brayer or wallpaper seam roller is used to roll over the print to make sure it is properly adhered to the surface and to press out air bubbles and wrinkles. You can find brayers at art supply stores, and wallpaper seam rollers at paint or home improvement stores. Wallpaper seam rollers are small enough to get into corners. Keep the brayer/roller clean; dried decoupage medium or glue on the brayer can damage papers.

TEXTURE, ANTIQUING, AND FINISHING SUPPLIES

Texture Medium: For best results when doing decoupage combined with texture medium, use a medium that has a fine to medium texture that is not thick. *See the discussion of "Texture Products" in the General Supplies chapter.*

Tools for Applying Texture:
• Palette knife, metal or plastic blade
• Putty knife
• Trowel
See the discussion of tools needed in the "Texturing Tools" section of the General Supplies chapter.

Paints:
Use acrylic paints for basecoating surfaces, adding color to areas of a project, and coloring glazes and antiquing mixtures.

Finishes:
Use a waterbased varnish for protecting dried, completed projects.

OTHER TOOLS & SUPPLIES

In addition to the tools and supplies you use for preparing the surface, applying texture, antiquing, and finishing, you will need:

- Cardboard scrap, for keeping your work surface clean. Place the print or paper face down on a piece of cardboard when applying decoupage medium/glue. Discard the cardboard after one use.
- Chip brushes, for applying decoupage medium, antiquing, and glazes.
- Foam brushes, for applying paints and decoupage medium to smooth surfaces. Textured surfaces may grind off bits of foam that will stick to your project.
- Artist's brushes, for painting details. Sizes: #8 filbert, #10 flat, #4 fan brush. Use a small round brush for tinting prints and photocopies.
- Palette, or plastic or foam plates or trays, for setting out and mixing mediums and paints.
- Water containers, one for rinsing brushes and one for clean water to thin paint or medium. You can use an artist's water basin or plastic margarine tubs.
- Paper shop towels or clean cloth rags, for cleanup, wiping glazes and antiquing.

- Painter's tape, for masking. To avoid lifting decoupaged papers, use a low tack masking tape and make sure the surface is completely dry before taping.
- Metal ruler, for measuring, using as a straightedge for cutting with a craft knife, or as an edge for tearing papers.
- Pencil, chalk pencil, and fine point marker, for marking, tracing or drawing.
- Scissors, for cutting paper, cardboard, fabric, or plastic.
- Craft knife and extra blades, for making intricate cuts. Change blades often; dull blades risk tearing rather than cutting the paper.
- Self-healing cutting mat, for protecting your work surface from craft knife cuts and prolonging the life of your blades.
- Damp cloth and baby wipes, for removing excess decoupage medium or glue from the project or your hands (keeping clean helps prevent accidentally tearing the paper). Cloth is safer to use on the decoupaged paper; baby wipes easily remove paint and medium/glue from your hands.
- Dishpan filled with water, for holding tools (not brushes) until you can clean them.
- Plastic tablecloth, for protecting your work area.

BASIC INSTRUCTIONS

PREPARING THE PRINT

- Cut Out or Tear the Print

Straight edges: Use a metal ruler, a craft knife with a sharp blade, and a self-healing cutting mat to cut straight edges. Square up the paper using the grid on the cutting mat. Each cut should be vertical. Place the center of the print on the same side as the hand that is holding the ruler, with the knife toward the side of the paper that will be discarded when it is trimmed off. That way, if your knife slips you won't cut into the part of the print you want to keep.

Be very sure the fingertips of the hand holding the ruler are well away from the path of the knife. Starting at the top and using your whole arm for the movement, pull the knife toward your body in a long, even stroke. Turn the paper so that each cut is made with maximum strength and control.

Rounded or irregular shapes: Cut with scissors in a freeform shape or follow the shape of an image printed on the paper.

Torn edges: For some projects, you may want the print to blend into the surface without noticeable lines made by the edges of the paper. Irregular torn edges soften the transition, and the loosened paper fibers will blend into the background and the texture when they are wet with decoupage medium.

Continued on page 32

BASIC INSTRUCTIONS

• Tinting

You can tint black and white photocopies or decoupage papers as well as black and white prints. Tint all or part of the print with the colors of your choice.

For a delicate watercolor look, apply thinned paint very lightly, so the black lines of the print show through. To get the effect of a hand-tinted photograph, make a copy of an old black and white photo and tint it with thinned acrylics.

1. Thin acrylic paints with water until the colors are transparent.
2. With a small artist's brush, add color to objects on the print.
3. Let the print dry thoroughly before you adhere it to the surface.

• Aging

To give your print or image the look of age:

1. Crumple the print or image, then flatten it out on your work surface.
2. Tear some of the edges or, if you are brave, tear a section out of the print.
3. Thin acrylic paint with water. Darken the torn edges and creases.
4. Let the print dry thoroughly before you adhere it to the surface.

• Sealing

Sealing the print before adhering it to the surface makes it easier to remove excess antiquing later on and protects the paper from accidental staining. This is personal preference. If you want to have ultimate control over the antiquing process, seal the paper first. You may choose not to seal when using an aging technique because the unevenness of the antiquing adds to the aged appearance.

1. Cut or tear the print to the desired size and shape.
2. Tint or age the print if desired.
3. Brush the front of the print with one or two coats of decoupage medium. Let dry after each coat.

APPLY THE PRINT

This is an artistic process so don't be afraid to experiment. If the paper tears it usually doesn't show in the finished project. If a tear bothers you, simply slap some texture medium over it in the next step.

To adhere the print to the surface:

1. Lay the image face down on a clean piece of cardboard. Apply an even coat of decoupage medium to the back with a brush, avoiding puddles and globs of excess medium.
2. Carefully lift the print and place it in position on the surface. Smooth from the center out to the edges with your fingers or a damp cloth to remove wrinkles and bubbles.
3. With a brayer, roll over the image in all directions to remove air bubbles and to make sure there is good contact between the paper and the surface.

Using a brayer to adhere the print. See the Da Vinci Woman project in this chapter for complete instructions.

4. Make certain that the edges have adhered by rubbing with your fingernail or a small wooden stirring stick.
5. Remove any excess decoupage medium with a damp cloth or paper towel.
6. Set aside to dry overnight.

TIPS:
- **Keep your hands and brayer clean.** Sticky hands can lift areas of the print.
- **Thick paper:** If you are working with thicker paper, apply an even coat of decoupage medium on both the paper and the surface before placing the print.
- **Large area:** If you are working with a large piece of paper, apply the decoupage medium to the center section, press and bray, apply medium to the next section, and so on until the entire sheet is adhered.
- **Textured surface:** It is important to ensure good contact when applying a print to a textured surface. You can expect some tearing, especially if you are using a thinner paper. It will just add to the aged look.
- **Bubbles and Wrinkles:** Bubbles occur when the decoupage medium dries before it adheres to the surface and a little pocket of air is trapped between the paper and the surface. You can dampen the paper first to keep the decoupage medium wet longer, but it also makes the paper more fragile and prone to tearing. Work out bubbles and wrinkles by smoothing and rolling from the center of the image out toward the edges. If you can't get the bubbles out, leave them alone. Many times they will disappear after the surface dries. If they remain, you can get rid of them by making a slit in the bubble with a sharp craft knife and putting decoupage medium under the paper with a small brush or toothpick. Flatten the area with a brayer.

APPLY TEXTURE MEDIUM

After the decoupaged print has dried completely, apply the texture medium with a palette knife, putty knife, or trowel. To marry the background surface, print, and texture, apply texture medium over the surface, overlapping the edges of the paper and part of the face of the print.

Brushstroke Texture
Sometimes you will not want opaque texture to cover your print. This technique gives the look of an old oil painting:

1. Apply a clear gel texture medium over the dried decoupaged print.
2. While the medium is wet, create a brushstroke texture with the palette knife or an artist's brush.
3. Let dry thoroughly.
4. Antique to bring out the brushstrokes.

CRACKLE SURFACE

For a crackled look, brush crackle medium over the project surface and the dried decoupaged paper at random, applying it thickly in some places and more thinly-or not at all-in other places. You can apply the crackle medium *before* or **after** you have applied the texture medium. Let the crackle medium dry.
If you have applied the crackle medium before the texture medium, apply the texture medium now. It will crackle as it dries. If you have applied the crackle medium on top of the texture medium, then add a top coat such as a varnish or a top coat that is specified for the crackle medium.

ANTIQUE

Antiquing your decoupage fresco will add richness to the colors and show off the textural effects. Make sure the texture is thoroughly dried and cured before antiquing. Refer to "Antiquing Methods" in *Chapter Two: Creating Textures.*
Apply and wipe back as much or as little of the antiquing color as you prefer. A deeply colored, substantial image may call for heavier antiquing, while an airy image may look better with lighter, more delicate antiquing.

Texture applied to tray. Antiquing has been applied on the right side. See the Autumn Vineyard Tray project in this chapter.

Autumn Vineyard Tray

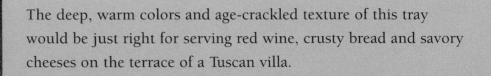

The deep, warm colors and age-crackled texture of this tray would be just right for serving red wine, crusty bread and savory cheeses on the terrace of a Tuscan villa.

SUPPLIES

Surface:

Wooden tray

Papers:

Wallpaper border, grapes & leaves pattern

Handmade papers, white, torn into irregular shapes

Texture:

Crackle texture

Acrylic Paints:

Arbor Green

Black

Burgundy

Burnt Umber

Raw Sienna

Red

Other Tools & Supplies:

Decoupage medium

Artist's fan brush, for dry brushing

Varnish

Gold metallic wax

INSTRUCTIONS

Preparation:

1. Prepare the surface as needed. Refer to "Preparing the Surface" in *Chapter 2: Creating Textures.*
2. Paint the tray with Red acrylic paint. Let dry.

Decoupage:

1. Use decoupage medium to adhere the torn handmade papers randomly to the inside of the tray. Let dry.
2. Cut the image from the wallpaper border.
3. Use decoupage medium to adhere the wallpaper image to the center of the tray. Roll with a brayer. Let dry. *(Photo 1)*

Apply Texture Medium:

Using a palette knife, apply areas of crackle texture over the inside of the tray and the image. *(Photo 2)* Let dry overnight.

Antique:

1. Thin a mixture of Burgundy + Black acrylic paint with water. Apply with a chip brush. *(Photo 3)*
2. Dry brush with Arbor Green acrylic paint. Let dry.
3. Dry brush with Raw Sienna acrylic paint. Let dry.

Finish:

1. Apply two or more coats of varnish, drying after each coat.
2. Rub gold metallic wax on the edges of the tray and on the surface of the texture. Buff with a soft cloth. ❑

Photo 1. Adhere the print to the surface with decoupage medium.

Photo 2. Apply crackle texture over part of the area.

Photo 3. Brush on the antiquing mixture of Burgundy + Black acrylic paints thinned with water.

Pieta Canvas Hanging

By Kathi Bailey

A crackled texture and mellow antiquing complement the meditative expression on this lovely face. When you select a print to use in this decoupage fresco technique, consider how the paint colors, texture, and antiquing processes you choose will enhance its emotional qualities.

SUPPLIES

Surface:
Canvas panel, 18" x 26"

Paper:
Print, 11" x 15"

Texture:
Venetian plaster, white

Acrylic Paints:
Asphaltum
Milkshake

Other Tools & Supplies:
Fabric glue
Decoupage medium
Crackle medium
Natural sponge, for antiquing
Sandpaper, 200 grit, for smoothing textured edges
Wooden rod and finials, for hanging the canvas
Varnish

INSTRUCTIONS

Preparation:
1. Turn under a ½" hem on all sides of canvas. Press to make a crease. Glue the hem down with fabric glue. Tape or put a weight on edges until glue is thoroughly dry.
2. To make a pocket at top for a rod, turn under 2" at the top of the canvas panel (or enough to accommodate the width of your rod). Glue the edge with fabric glue. Let dry thoroughly.
3. Basecoat the canvas panel with two coats of Milkshake acrylic paint. Let dry after each coat.

Decoupage:
1. Hand tear the edges of the print so that you have not straight edges. This will help the print to better meld into the canvas surface.
2. Seal the front of the print with decoupage medium. Let dry.
3. Center the print on the canvas, measuring and marking lightly with a pencil.
4. Coat the back of the print with decoupage medium. Adhere to the center of the canvas panel at the marks. Press with a dampened sponge or use a brayer to make sure the print is adhered without air bubbles.
5. Apply a second coat of decoupage medium to the front of the print. Let dry.

Apply Texture Medium:
1. Use a foam brush to apply crackle medium on the canvas and on the print where you want it to be crackled. Let dry.
2. Use a putty knife to apply a top coat of Venetian plaster over the canvas and over the edges of the print. Also apply some to sections of the print. The plaster will crackle as it dries where it has come in contact with the crackle medium. Let dry thoroughly.
3. If needed, you can smooth some of the textured areas by sanding lightly.

Apply Varnish:
Use a foam brush to apply varnish over the entire surface. This will crackle additional areas where crackle medium has been applied. Let dry.

Antique:
1. Mix 1 part Asphaltum acrylic paint with 2 to 3 parts water on a plate. Dampen the sponge and dip it into the mixture. Wipe over the surface to reveal the cracks. Let dry.
2. Replaster, antique, and sand as desired.

Finish:
1. Seal with a coat of varnish. Let dry.
2. Insert the rod through the pocket at the top of the canvas. ❏

Aurora Canvas Hanging

By Kathi Bailey

The technique used to create this canvas is the same as the Pieta Canvas. Follow those instructions to create a decoupage fresco that celebrates the classic beauty of an ancient Greek goddess.

Classic Floral Frescoes

By Kathi Bailey
People have decorated their homes with delicate floral paintings for thousands of years, and they delight us as much as they delighted the citizens of imperial Rome. These fresco blossoms bear their history lightly, with just enough texture to emphasize their timeless beauty.

See Pages 40 & 41 for instructions and additional photos.

Classic Floral Frescoes
Continued from page 39

SUPPLIES

Surfaces:
3 Pre-stretched canvases,
    11" x 14"

Papers:
3 Floral prints, 8" x 10"

Texture:
Venetian plaster, white

Acrylic Paints:
Taffy
Yellow Ochre

Other Tools & Supplies:
Decoupage medium
Crackle medium
Premixed antiquing glaze, brown
Natural sponge, for antiquing
Sandpaper, 200 grit, for smoothing
    texture
Varnish

INSTRUCTIONS

Preparation:
1. Basecoat the canvas with one coat of Taffy acrylic paint. Let dry. Sand surface lightly.
2. Apply a second coat of paint. Let dry.

Decoupage:
1. Tear the edges of the print by hand so remove any straight edges.
2. Seal the front of the print with decoupage medium. Let dry.
3. Center the print on the canvas, measuring and marking lightly with a pencil.
4. Coat the back of the print with decoupage medium. Adhere to the center of the canvas panel at the marks. Press carefully with a dampened sponge or use a brayer to make sure the print is adhered without air bubbles.
5. Apply a second coat of decoupage medium to the front of the print. Let dry.

Apply Crackle Medium:
Use a foam brush to apply crackle medium on the surface of the canvas and on the print in area where you want there to be a crackle texture. Let dry.

Apply Texture Medium:
Use a putty knife to apply a topcoat of Venetian plaster randomly over the canvas and edges of the print. As the plaster dries, it will crackle in the areas where it has been applied over the crackle medium. Let dry thoroughly.

Apply Varnish:
Use a foam brush to apply varnish over the entire surface. This will crackle additional areas where crackle medium has been applied. Let dry.

Antique:
1. Mix 1 part Yellow Ochre acrylic paint with 2 to 3 parts water on a plate. Dampen the sponge and dip it into the mixture. Wipe over the surface to reveal the cracks. Let dry.
2. Apply brown antiquing glaze over random areas. Let dry.

Finish:
Apply two or more coats of varnish, drying after each coat. ❑

Fruits & Vines Book Cover

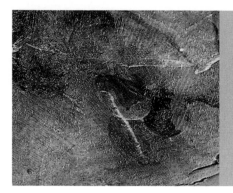

Images of sun-warmed, ripe fruits and vine leaves evoke a harvest of thoughts and memories: keep a journal, record your dreams, or set down your favorite recipes. Use the decoupage fresco technique to rejuvenate an old address or recipe book or to decorate a new book to your taste.

SUPPLIES

Surface:
Canvas-covered book

Paper:
Wallpaper border

Texture:
Tinted texture medium, Natural

Acrylic Paint:
Burnt Umber

Other Tools & Supplies:
Decoupage medium
Varnish

INSTRUCTIONS

Decoupage:

1. Cut the wallpaper border so that it wraps around the book with enough extra length to wrap and glue inside the book for a nice finished edge.

2. Seal the front of the wallpaper border with decoupage medium. Let dry.

3. Coat the back of the wallpaper border with decoupage medium. Adhere to the book cover. Use a brayer to make sure the print is adhered without air bubbles. Let dry.

4. Apply a second coat of decoupage medium to the front of the wallpaper border. Let dry.

Apply Texture Medium:

Apply the texture medium to the book cover with a palette knife, overlapping the wallpaper in some areas. Let dry.

Antique:

1. Thin Burnt Umber acrylic paint with water. Apply with a chip brush.

2. Wipe back with a soft cloth or paper towel. Let dry.

Finish:

Apply one or two coats of varnish, drying after each coat. ❑

Angel Photo Box

With prints, paints, and stucco, you can transform a utilitarian box into an archive for romantic photographs and keepsakes. This would make a lovely gift for a bride-to-be.

SUPPLIES

Surface:
Photo box

Paper:
Black & white image of angel

Texture:
Tinted stucco, Dusty Rose

Acrylic Paints:
Burgundy
Burnt Umber
Pink
Assorted colors for tinting the print

Other Tools & Supplies:
Decoupage medium
Small round artist's brush, for tinting the print
Natural sponge, for smoothing decoupaged images
Varnish

INSTRUCTIONS

Preparation:
You may tint the print before or after adhering it to the box. Do not seal the front of the print until you have finished coloring it.
1. Tint the print, using the artist's brush and acrylic paints thinned with water. For a delicate watercolor effect, use very thin paint and apply it lightly so the black lines show through. For a hand-tinted photo effect, photocopy an old black & white photo and color it subtly with acrylics. Let the paint dry.
2. Basecoat the box with two coats of Pink acrylic paint. Let dry after each coat.

The cutout print has been adhered to the box with decoupage medium.

Decoupage:
1. Cut out the print, if desired. Seal the front of the print with decoupage medium. Let dry.
2. Coat the back of the print with decoupage medium. Adhere to the box lid. Use a brayer to make sure the print is adhered without air bubbles. Let dry.
3. Apply a second coat of decoupage medium to the front of the print. Let dry.

Apply Texture Medium:
1. Apply Dusty Rose stucco to the outside of the box and lid with a palette knife, overlapping the image in some places. Apply thinly to the sides of the box—if it is too thick the lid will no longer fit.
2. Wipe back some of the stucco over the image.
3. Texture the stucco with plastic wrap. Let dry. (Refer to "Using Tools to Create Texture" in *Chapter 2: Creating Textures.*)

Antique:
1. Mix Burnt Umber + Burgundy acrylic paints to create a brownish rose color. Thin with water to create an antiquing glaze. Apply with a chip brush.
2. Wipe back with a soft cloth or paper towel. Let dry.

Finish:
Apply one or two coats of varnish, drying after each coat. ❑

Elegant Floral Cachepot

Train your artist's eye to notice basic shapes when you are choosing prints for specific surfaces to decorate. The flaring shape of this planter echoes the fan-like shape of the urn and flowers in the print, and the arc above the floral arrangement completes the harmonious repetition of shapes. Elegant design involves more than beautiful colors and rich textures.

SUPPLIES

Surface:
Metal planter box

Papers:
Prints for all 4 sides

Texture:
Texture medium

Acrylic Paints:
Burnt Umber
Black Forest Green

Other Tools & Supplies:
Decoupage medium
Crackle medium
Clear wax

INSTRUCTIONS

Preparation:
Prepare the surface as needed. Refer to "Preparing the Surface" in *Chapter 2: Creating Textures.*

Decoupage:
1. Tear or cut the prints to the desired size.
2. Seal the fronts of the prints with decoupage medium. Let dry.
3. Adhere the prints to the planter one at a time, working while the decoupage medium is wet. Coat the back of the print with decoupage medium. Adhere to the side of the planter. Rub down carefully and roll with a brayer to make sure the print is adhered without air bubbles. Let dry.
4. Apply a second coat of decoupage medium to the fronts of the prints. Let dry.

Apply Texture Medium:
Using a palette knife, apply texture to the sides of the planter, partially overlapping the prints, and manipulate the texture with your choice of methods. Let dry.

Apply Crackle Medium:
1. Apply crackle medium with a soft brush to all four sides. Let dry.
2. Apply a coat of varnish to create the crackle texture. Let dry.

Antique:
1. Thin Black Forest Green acrylic paint with water. Brush over the sides of the planter.
2. Wipe back with a soft cloth or paper towel. Let dry.
3. Add additional antiquing with thinned Burnt Umber. Let dry.

Finish:
Apply a coat of wax. Buff. ❑

Photo 1: Photo shows print adhered to surface of planter.

Photo 2: Texture medium has been applied to cover sections of print.

Photo 3: Antiquing has been applied.

Da Vinci Woman Canvas

A print of Leonardo's masterful drawing deserves star treatment! Apply texture and antiquing to enhance the warm colors of the print and emphasize the timeless beauty of the dreaming subject.

SUPPLIES

Surface:
Canvas board the size of your poster

Paper:
Old Master poster or print

Texture:
Texture medium

Acrylic Paint:
Burnt Umber

Other Tools & Supplies:
Decoupage medium
Varnish

INSTRUCTIONS

Apply Texture Medium:
Using a palette knife, apply texture medium to the surface of the canvas board. Let dry.

Decoupage:
Refer to the "Apply the Print" section

of this chapter for instructions for working with thick paper and large pieces of paper.

1. Seal the front of the print with decoupage medium. Let dry.
2. Coat the back of the print with decoupage medium. Adhere to the canvas board. Roll with a brayer to make sure the print is adhered and melds with the texture. *(Photo 1)* Let dry.
3. Apply a second coat of decoupage medium to the front of the print. Let dry.

Apply Texture Medium:
Using a palette knife, apply texture medium to the edges and surface of the poster. *(Photo 2)* Let dry.

Antique:
1. Thin Burnt Umber acrylic paint with water. Brush over the surface with a chip brush.
2. Wipe back with a soft cloth or paper towel. Let dry.

Finish:
Apply one or two coats of varnish, drying after each coat. ❑

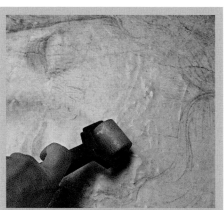

Photo 1. Adhering the print.

Photo 2. Apply texture to cover sections of the print.

Impressionist Painting

Do you crave juicy, jazzy color? Do you feel spontaneous and energetic? Start with a photocopied magazine photo, add texture and paint, and create your own Impressionist canvas.

SUPPLIES

Surface:
Stretched canvas, 11" x 14"

Paper:
Color photocopy of a magazine photo

Texture:
Texture medium

Acrylic Paints:
Black
Black Forest Green
Burnt Umber
Green
Red
Yellow

Other Tools & Supplies:
Decoupage medium
Varnish (optional)

INSTRUCTIONS

Decoupage:
1. Make a color photocopy of a photo or magazine image that has strong diagonal lines like the tree trunks in the example.
2. Seal the front of the copy with decoupage medium. Let dry.
3. Coat the back of the copy with decoupage medium. Adhere to the stretched canvas. Smooth down and roll with a brayer to make sure it is adhered without air bubbles. Let dry.
4. Apply a second coat of decoupage medium to the front of the copy. Let dry.

Apply Texture Medium:
Using a palette knife, apply texture medium to the surface of the image to imitate bark. *(Photo 2)* Let dry.

Apply Paint:
At this point you could antique the surface and have a dimensional picture. To create a strong abstract design, apply acrylic colors in areas of the image; it is not necessary to cover the image completely. The example shows reds and yellow in the central opening between the trees and greens and black on the vertical and diagonal shapes made by the tree trunks. *(Photo 2)* Let dry.

Apply Texture Medium:
Apply additional texture with the palette knife, pulling over the painting in the opposite diagonal. Let dry.

Antique:
1. Thin Burnt Umber acrylic paint with water. Brush over the surface with a chip brush.
2. Wipe back with a soft cloth or paper towel. Let dry.

Photo 1. This photo was the starting point.

Photo 2. Texture medium applied to tree trunks.

Finish:
Apply one or two coats of varnish if desired, drying after each coat. ❑

Garden Trellis Canvas

A poster of a painting by JW Waterhouse, "The Soul of the Rose," inspired this design, and is its focal point. Any image showing a garden would be lovely viewed through the door in the very dimensional trellis. The vines on the trellis were created by applying texture medium through a stencil.

SUPPLIES

Surface:
Stretched canvas, 15" x 30"(or the size of your print)

Paper:
Print or poster

Texture:
Texture medium (stucco or model-ing paste)
Clear gel texture medium

Acrylic Paints:
Arbor Green
Black Forest Green
Burnt Sienna
Burnt Umber
Evergreen Black
Light Avocado

Other Tools & Supplies:
Decoupage medium
Artist's brush, #10 filbert
Stencil, ivy or trailing flowers
Removable address labels, 1" x 2" and cut in half, for masking trellis openings (or use 1" wide masking tape)

INSTRUCTIONS

Decoupage:
1. Cut the print to 12½" x 23", using a craft knife, metal ruler, and cutting mat. Use a sharp blade to avoid tearing the paper.
2. Seal the front of the print with decoupage medium. Let dry.
3. Coat the back of the print with decoupage medium. Adhere to the lower right of the stretched canvas. Smooth out air bubbles and wrinkles. Let dry.

Background Painting:
Paint the remainder of the canvas to give the illusion of background foliage seen through the texture trellis.
1. Squeeze out onto your palette green acrylic paints to match some of the background greens in the print.
2. Starting next to the print and overlapping the print, apply green shades of paint with random brushstrokes, slip-slapping in an X motion with the artist's brush and applying colors over each other. Where the print color is darker apply the darker greens; where it is lighter choose the green that is the nearest match. *(Photo 1 and Photo 2)*
3. Paint the remainder of the canvas with a green foliage-like background. Let dry overnight.

Photo 1. *Begin filling in the background painting at the edge of the print.*

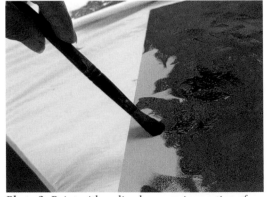

Photo 2. *Paint with a slip-slap, crossing motion of the brush.*

Continued on page 54

Garden Trellis Canvas

Continued from page 52

Trellis:

The painted canvas and decoupage medium must be thoroughly dry or you will risk lifting areas of the print.

1. Apply painter's tape along the top and side of the print to protect it from the texture medium.
2. Measure and draw vertical and horizontal lines with a chalk pencil on the painted canvas. Make the trellis 1¼" and the opening 1".
3. Place the removable address label halves on the canvas to mask the openings in the trellis. Or use 1" wide masking tape, cut into 1" sections. *(Photo 3)*
4. Using a palette knife, apply texture medium to the trellis area only.
5. Immediately remove the labels with a clean palette knife. Do not allow the labels to dry into the texture. *(Photo 4)* Let dry.

Antique the Trellis:

1. Antique the trellis with thinned Burnt Sienna and thinned Burnt Umber. Apply with a chip brush.
2. Wipe back with a soft cloth or paper towel. Let dry.*(Photo 5)*

Leaves:

Refer to "Using the Stencil" in Chapter 4: Texturing with Stencils.

1. Position the leaf stencil and secure it in place with painter's tape.
2. With a palette knife, apply texture medium to the stencil. Remove the stencil carefully.
3. Wipe the stencil with a paper towel. Secure in the next position, far enough away from the previously stenciled leaves to

Photo 3. Place masking tape or labels over the areas that will be the openings of the trellis.

Photo 4. Apply texture medium to canvas. Remove the labels to reveal the painted background.

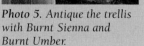

Photo 5. Antique the trellis with Burnt Sienna and Burnt Umber.

Photo 6. Stencil the leaf design.

Photo 7. Paint the leaves with thinned green acrylic paint.

avoid smearing the wet stenciled texture.

4. Repeat until all the leaves have been stenciled. Let dry. *(Photo 6)*
5. To build up the thickness of the leaves, position the stencil over the dried leaves and apply a second layer of texture medium, following the same procedure as the first stenciled layer. Let dry.
6. Paint the leaves with green acrylic paint thinned with water. *(Photo 7)*

Brush Strokes & Antiquing:

Add brush stroke texture to the print by applying clear gel texture medium with an artist's brush. Follow the brush strokes you see in the print. For flatter areas without detail, just use random X motions of the brush.

Antique:

1. Thin Black Forest Green with water. Apply over the entire piece with a chip brush.
2. Wipe back with a soft cloth or paper towel. Let dry.

Finish:

Apply one or two coats of varnish, drying after each coat. ❏

CHAPTER 4

Texturing with Stencils

Stencils have a long tradition in home decoration because they work so well and give good results on many surfaces – walls, floors, canvas, and fabrics.

The popularity of stenciling means there are pre-cut stencils in many designs, and they are readily available at home decor centers and paint stores as well as art and craft stores. Stencils made from plastic materials are more durable, and can be washed and used again and again.

You can also design and cut your own stencils following the instructions in this chapter. If your project incorporates a print, an element from the image would be a good starting point for your design, and the repetition of shapes and themes will help unify the canvas or project.

SUPPLIES

PRE-CUT STENCILS

Many stencil designs are available at home decor centers, paint stores, and art and craft stores. Plastic stencil material is more durable for use with texture mediums; it can be wiped, washed, and used multiple times.

TOOLS & SUPPLIES FOR CUTTING STENCILS

Stencil blank material: This can be plastic, acetate, cardboard, or manila file folders. Thicker materials will require two or more passes with the knife and may increase the chance for cutting errors, but can give you more of a raised design when using texture medium. Plastic materials are durable, while paper and cardstock can disintegrate when they are wet.

Craft knives: Cutting stencils requires a very sharp blade. To cut larger shapes, use a knife with blades that snap off to provide a new, sharp edge. For details, use a knife with replaceable blades, and keep plenty of extra blades on hand.

Self-healing cutting mat: Use for protecting your work surface from craft knife cuts and prolonging the life of your blades.

Metal ruler, for measuring and as a guide for cutting straight pieces of the stencil design. You may also use a wooden ruler with a metal edge.

Stencil burner: Used for cutting plastic blank materials, the fine-tipped metal point of an electric stencil burner gets as hot as 600 degrees Fahrenheit. Follow the manufacturer's use and safety instructions.

Glass cutting surface: If you use a stencil burner, you must use a piece of glass as a cutting surface, to produce a clean cut and to protect your work surface from heat damage.

TOOLS & SUPPLIES FOR USING STENCILS

Stencil adhesive: Spray on the back of the stencil. It will hold the stencil in place so it does not move while you are working. This is best used on a design that has a lot of small cutout areas.

Painter's tape, for holding the stencil in place, masking the surface, and blocking parts of the stencil you choose not to use. Use a low tack tape and make sure the surface is dry before applying, to avoid lifting parts of the texture.

Removable adhesive dots, letters or other shapes; removable address labels: These make good negative stencils and masks. Adhere to the surface before applying texture medium. Remove before the texture medium dries to reveal areas of the surface surrounded by texture.

TEXTURE, ANTIQUING, AND FINISHING SUPPLIES

Texture Medium: For best results when doing stenciling combined with texture medium, use a medium that has a fine to medium texture and that is not thick. *See the discussion of "Texture Products" in the General Supplies chapter.*

Tools for Applying Texture:
• Palette knife, metal or plastic blade
• Putty knife
• Trowel
See the discussion of tools needed in the "Texturing Tools" section of the General Supplies chapter.

Paints:
Use acrylic paints for basecoating surfaces, adding color to areas of a project, and coloring glazes and antiquing mixtures.

Finishes:
Use a waterbased varnish for protecting dried, completed projects.

OTHER TOOLS & SUPPLIES

In addition to the tools and supplies you use for preparing the surface, applying texture, antiquing, and finishing, you will need:
• Chip brushes, for applying paints, antiquing, and glazes.
• Foam brushes, for applying paints and finishes to smooth surfaces. Textured surfaces may grind off bits of foam that will stick to your project.
• Artist's brushes, for painting details.
• Palette, or plastic or foam plates or trays, for setting out and mixing mediums and paints.
• Water containers, one for rinsing brushes and one for clean water to thin paint or medium. You can use an artist's water basin or plastic margarine tubs.
• Paper shop towels or clean cloth rags, for cleanup, wiping glazes and antiquing.
• Pencil, chalk pencil, and fine point marker, for marking, tracing or drawing.
• Scissors, for cutting paper, cardboard, fabric, or plastic.
• Baby wipes, for cleaning your hands.
• Dishpan filled with water, for holding tools (not brushes) until you can clean them.
• Plastic tablecloth, for protecting your work area.

BASIC INSTRUCTIONS

DESIGNING A STENCIL

You can use patterns from this or other books, look for free stencil designs on the internet, or create an original design.

Your idea can come from your own sketches, from motifs or lettering that have significance for the recipient if you are creating a gift, or from an element on a print you are using in the project. For example, a shape from the wallpaper border of the "Seek Truth Banner" in this chapter could be the basis of a stencil design.

Developing your design:

- Remember that the area that is cut out will be the raised or relief area of the design. You can use a black marker to help you see that more clearly.
- Stencil designs have *bridges,* which are the 1/8-inch-wide sections between the cutout shapes that hold the stencil together and give the stencil extra strength. All areas or *islands* within your design must be connected by bridges. Look at precut stencils to see how bridges are used as design elements in their own right.
- If you do not like the look of stencil bridges in a particular project, you can cut out multiple stencil overlays for the design. See the "Here Comes the Sun Stepping Stone" project for an example.
- Remember that larger, simple designs are easier to cut than tiny, intricate designs, and are more suitable for heavy textures.
- Work out your design on paper, including all the bridges. Tracing paper is useful for figuring out the placement of cutout shapes and bridges.

- Make a final tracing with a fine point black marker. Enlarge or reduce your design on a photocopier.

Using your computer for lettering designs:

- Type out a name or phrase, select a font and size, and print out the page.
- You can make a monogram from initials. When you have an arrangement you like, print out the page.
- Enlarge or reduce your lettering design on a photocopier.

CUTTING A STENCIL

Make a copy of your original design since it may be damaged during the cutting process.

Stencil materials

When you choose stencil materials, consider the textural or paint effect you want to achieve, the ease of cutting, and the durability of the material.

- Stencil materials include commercial stencil paper, heavy cardstock, cardboard, manila file folders, transparent plastic material, template plastic, acetate, or craft foam.
- The thickness of the stencil material will create the thickness of the relief.
- Thinner paper materials are easier to cut but may not stand up to multiple uses. If you will be using the stencil more than once or twice, use a more durable material.

Cutting a Stencil with a Craft Knife:

- Avoid ragged edges and tears by always using a sharp blade.
- Use a craft knife that has snap-off blades for cutting larger or simpler shapes.

- Use a craft knife with a pencil-thin handle and replaceable fine-pointed blades for cutting out details and intricate curves. Hold it like a pencil and draw the blade along the design.
- Protect your work surface with a self-healing mat (which will make your blades last longer), a piece of glass, a cutting board, or other thick material.

Cutting a Stencil with a Stencil Burner:

- Use for cutting plastic materials quickly and smoothly.
- You *must* use a piece of glass as a cutting surface.
- Hold the wooden handle as if it were a pencil and follow the pattern lines to cut your stencil.
- Follow the manufacturer's safety instructions. Be sure you have a heat-proof rest for the hot tool, and be careful not to touch the tip.
- Follow the manufacturer's recommendations for stencil materials; the stencil burner does not work for some plastic materials.

Cut the Stencil

1. Use a piece of stencil blank material at least 1" larger than your design on all sides.
2. If you are using a clear material, tape the stencil design to the cutting surface and place the material on top of the design. If you use glass to protect the work surface, slide the design under the glass. If you are using foam or other opaque material, tape the design to the top of the material.
3. Tape the stencil material to the cutting surface. If the pattern and stencil materials are secured in place it is less likely that something will slip while you are cutting.

4. Begin by cutting along the longest, straightest edges of the design; these are the easiest lines to cut. Pulling the knife toward you, press firmly and smoothly with the blade and use your free hand to hold the stencil material in place. Turn your work or reposition yourself so you are always holding the knife at a comfortable angle and pulling toward your body.

5. When the entire design has been cut out, smooth any rough edges with sandpaper or a nail file.

USING THE STENCIL

Preparation

Photo 1

Photo 2

Photo 3

- You can use the entire stencil or just a portion of it. Place masking tape over the unwanted areas.
- Secure the stencil to the surface with masking tape or stencil adhesive. If the stencil is small you can hold it in place with your hand. *(Photo 1)*

Applying Texture

- With a palette knife, apply texture to the surface of the stencil, filling in the area but being careful not to work the texture medium under the stencil. *(Photo 2)* Scrape off the excess material and put it back into the jar.
- You can use any of the texturizing techniques while the stencil is still in place.
- Gently peel the stencil back and lift it off. *(Photo 3)*
- You can build up or overlap areas of texture. When one application of texture has dried, reapply the stencil and add another layer of texture medium.
- If you are using the stencil more than once you may need to clean it between applications of texture. Use a palette knife or clean brush to remove excess texture. Wipe with a paper towel or cloth.

Using Masks or Negative Stencils

You can use masks to keep texture from adhering to the surface wherever you want the background to show through. Use the shapes you cut out of your stencil design; removable adhesive letters, dots, shapes, and address labels; or masking tape. Stick them to the surface, apply the texture medium, and remove the masks at once with a palette knife. Do not allow the texture to dry in place or the masks will be difficult to remove. Removable adhesive address labels were used as masks to create the trellis openings in the "Garden Trellis" project in *Chapter 3: Decoupage Frescoes.*

Adding Color to Stenciled Texture

When your stenciled area is dry, you can enhance the raised area with paint, antiquing and/or dry brushing. You can also mix colorants into the texture medium before applying it to the stencil. (Refer to "Tinting Texture Medium" in *Chapter 2: Creating Textures.*)

CARING FOR STENCILS

- Keep the stencil clean so it can be used multiple times.
- Place the plastic or foam stencil (and your palette knife) in a dishpan filled with water immediately after you use it to keep the texture or paint from drying permanently on the stencil. There is not always time to clean up while working on your project.
- Wash plastic or foam stencils with soap and water.
- Remove texture medium from paper or cardboard stencils with a clean palette knife or brush.
- Dry thoroughly and store flat.
- To keep the stencil from becoming distorted, store it between two pieces of cardboard. Keep the backing board that comes with the stencil for this purpose.

Iris & Butterflies Buffet

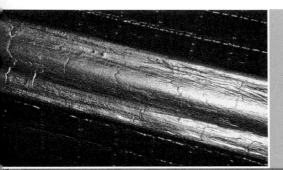

By Rose Wilde

Textures, stenciled designs, and lovingly applied finishes transformed a flea market dresser into this proudly unique dining room buffet. The stenciled iris and butterfly designs were stained to look like carved wood embellishments.

SUPPLIES

Surface:

Wooden dresser

Texture:

Texture medium

Paints:

Latex paint for basecoating, dark
chocolate brown

Tan acrylic paint

Other Tools & Supplies:

Crackle medium

Grid stencil

Pre-cut iris stencil

Pre-cut butterfly & tree branch
stencil

Small round artist's brush, for
touching up details

Spray bottle filled with water, for
misting surfaces

Primer (if needed), for preparing
the surface

Wood stain, mahogany color

Waterbased polyurethane varnish,
clear

Before

MEET ROSE WILDE

Rose is the inventor of the Wood Icing technique and the
manufacturer of Wood Icing™ product. After many years of creative
exploration, Rose felt that readily available products used to strip,
paint, and reconstruct flea market finds weren't able to deliver the
results that fulfilled her vision for these treasures.

The technique and product she developed delivered unique,
versatile, and durable effects. She made piece after piece, impressing
her friends and family and newfound clients. The word spread
quickly, and soon she received client
referrals and calls from decorators asking
for custom pieces. The response to her
product and technique has been over-
whelming. Rose and her husband Jack
manage the company full time. Rose still
spends countless hours in her "Rose Wilde
Design Studio" creating new techniques
and ways to use the product. She also
travels throughout the United States
teaching her technique with her products.

*Rose Wilde, President
The Wood Icing Company*

INSTRUCTIONS

Preparation:

1. There is no need to strip old paint. Scrape off loose particles, then sand
   to roughen the surface.

2. Wash the surface with a heavy duty cleaning product that contains
   trisodium phosphate (TSP). Wear rubber gloves and follow the
   manufacturer's safety instructions. Let dry.

3. Make any necessary repairs.

4. If the remaining old paint still flakes off, or can be pulled off with tape,
   apply primer. Choose a primer appropriate for the surface; in this project,
   a primer made to cover shiny surfaces was used. Let dry. *(Photo 1)*

5. Basecoat the entire piece with dark chocolate brown paint. Let dry.
   (Photo 2)

Continued on next page

Photo 1. Applying primer.

Photo 2. Applying the basecoat.

IRIS & BUTTERFLIES BUFFET
Continued from page 61

Apply Crackle Medium:

Brush crackle medium on the side trim and bottom legs of the buffet. *(Photo 3)*

Photo 3. Applying crackle medium to the trim.

Apply Texture Medium:

1. Working in small sections at a time, apply the texture medium and smooth the surface with a trowel. *(Photo 4)*

2. Spray with a very fine mist of water if the texture medium is dragging as you spread it. Do not use too much water, or the heavy texture will slide and sag on vertical surfaces.

Photo 4. Applying texture medium with a trowel.

Add Grid Texture:

1. Dampen the grid stencil. *(Photo 5)* Lay it in place. Press the grid design into the texture medium, using a light touch with the trowel. *(Photo 6)* Carefully peel up the grid stencil.

2. Spread texture medium on the next section and press the grid stencil into the medium. Repeat until all surfaces are covered with the grid design. To keep grid lines straight, place the grid stencil overlapping into the previous lines.

Apply Texture to Trim:

1. Apply texture medium to the trim areas you painted with crackle medium. Use your fingers to smooth the texture medium into grooved areas, or thin the texture medium with a little water and apply it with a brush.

2. The texture medium will crackle as it dries.

Photo 5. Spraying the grid stencil lightly with water.

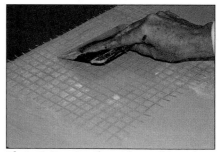

Photo 6. Pressing the grid stencil into the texture medium.

Apply Stain & Polyurethane:

1. Allow the piece to dry overnight to a hard, crisp surface.

2. Smooth and clean up all surfaces by sanding with medium to fine grit sandpaper or sanding block. Wear a mask while sanding. Vacuum all dust away and wipe with a damp cloth before applying the stain.

3. Apply wood conditioner to promote uniform stain absorption over large surfaces. Let dry according to the manufacturer's instructions.

4. Apply wood stain to entire piece of furniture. Allow to dry thoroughly. (Photo 7)

5. Apply one coat of polyurethane. Let dry. Photo 8) This will act as a barrier coat to the lighter paint that will be applied to the stenciled iris designs. You can get away with this because the grid patterned texture will still allow the next layer of texture medium to adhere to the surface.

Photo 7. Brushing on the stain.

Photo 8. Applying polyurethane.

Photo 9. Taping the stencil in place.

Stencil the Designs:

1. Tape the iris stencil in place over the dried surface. (Photo 9)

2. Trowel texture medium through the stencil. Use a light, even touch, and avoid letting the stencil lift during the application so as to prevent the texture medium from bleeding out beyond the design. Carefully lift off the stencil. Repeat until you complete all the stenciled designs.

3. To maintain the continuous design going from one drawer to the next, place the drawers together and stencil the design. Remove the stencil. Slice through the design with a clean palette knife while the texture medium is wet. (Photo 10)

4. When the stenciled texture has dried thoroughly, sand off the high spots and clean up the surface. (Photo 11) Vacuum away the sanding dust and wipe with a damp cloth.

5. Using a small round artist's brush, touch up the edges of the design with the previous color. Let dry. (Photo 12)

6. Apply tan acrylic paint over the iris stenciled design, manipulating the color with a dry brush. Once you have achieved the color you desire, let dry. (Photo 13)

Finish:

When all the paint is thoroughly dry, apply three or more coats of polyurethane varnish, drying after each coat. ❏

Photo 10. Slicing through the wet stenciled texture between drawers.

Photo 11. Sanding the stenciled design.

Photo 12. Touching up the edges of the stenciled design.

Photo 13. Applying the light color over the stenciled design with a dry brush.

Seek Truth Banner

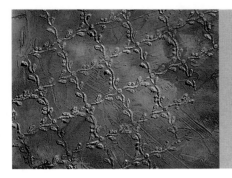

There is no rule that says wise words must look boring. Why not use your creative talents to draw the eye and attract thoughtful attention to an inspirational message? You could use your computer to print out a message of your own, and cut a stencil for applying texture.

SUPPLIES

Surface:
Canvas floor cloth or unmounted canvas, 24" x 36"

Paper for Decoupage:
Wallpaper border, your choice

Stencils:
Pre-cut stencil in a trellis grid pattern
Seek Truth stencil, cut using the pattern provided

Textures:
Clear gel texture medium
Fine texture medium
Stucco

Acrylic Paints:
Burgundy
Burnt Umber
Buttermilk
Glazing medium

Other Tools & Supplies:
Decoupage medium
Brayer, for rolling down decoupaged paper
Artist's fan brush, for dry brushing
Fabric glue
Decorative rod

INSTRUCTIONS

Cut the Stencil:
Refer to the stencil cutting instructions at the beginning of this chapter.
1. Photocopy the "Seek Truth" pattern. Enlarge or reduce the pattern if needed.
2. Trace the pattern onto stencil blank material using a fine point marker.
3. Cut out the stencil with a craft knife or stencil burner.

Decoupage:
1. Measure 6" down from the top of the canvas and draw a horizontal line.
2. Seal the front of the wallpaper border with decoupage medium. Let dry.
3. Coat the back of the wallpaper border with decoupage medium.
4. Adhere the wallpaper border to the canvas, lining up the top of the wallpaper border on the horizontal line. Rub down, then roll with a brayer to flatten air bubbles. Let dry.

Apply Texture Medium:
With a palette knife, apply stucco to the entire surface of the canvas below the border. Let dry.

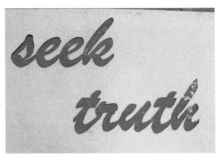

Photo 1. Stencil in position.

Photo 2. Texture medium applied over the stencil.

Photo 3. Stenciled texture designs before antiquing.

Continued on page 66

Seek Truth Banner

Continued from page 64

Stencil the Designs:

1. Position the stencils for the words and secure it in place with masking tape. *(Photo 1)*
2. With a palette knife, apply fine texture medium to the stencil. *(Photo 2)* Remove the stencil carefully. Let dry. *(Photo 3)*
3. Position the trellis stencil and secure it in place with masking tape.
4. With a palette knife, apply fine texture medium to the stencil. Remove the stencil carefully.
5. Reposition the trellis stencil and add fine texture medium two more times.

Apply Clear Gel Texture Medium:

With a palette knife, apply clear gel texture medium to the wallpaper border. Let dry.

Antique:

1. Mix Burgundy and Burnt Umber acrylic paints to make a dark rose color. Thin this mixture with glazing medium. Apply over the entire banner, including the area above the wallpaper border.
2. Using a paper towel, blot off some areas of the antiquing in a random pattern. Let dry.
3. Using the fan brush and Buttermilk colored acrylic paint, dry brush the stenciled designs.

Finish:

1. Create a pocket for the rod by folding over the top of the canvas and gluing on the back with fabric glue. Add weight to hold the folded canvas flat until the glue dries.
2. Insert the rod. ❑

Stencil Pattern

(actual size)

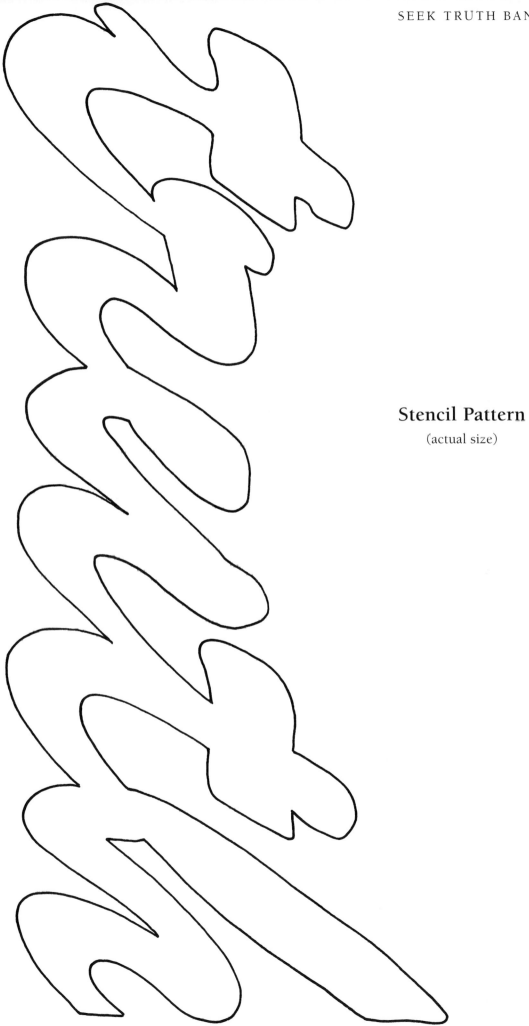

Stencil Pattern

(actual size)

Pear Orchard Cabinet Door

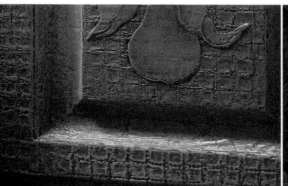

By Rose Wilde

The pear-stenciled cabinet door was created with the "shabby chic" decorating style in mind. Cabinets aren't just for kitchens.

This door treatment would look wonderful on a hutch in the dining room or an entertainment center in a family room.

SUPPLIES

Surface:

Paneled cabinet door

Texture:

Texture medium

Paints:

Latex paint for basecoat, dark
   chocolate color

White satin latex paint or white
   acrylic paint

Other Tools & Supplies:

Crackle medium

Pre-cut pear & leaves stencil with
   2 stencil overlays

Grid stencil

Small paint rollers (optional), for
   applying crackle medium,
   primer, or paint

Spray bottle filled with water, for
   misting surfaces

Sandpaper, for smoothing texture

Small round artist's brush, for
   touching up antiquing

Primer (if needed)

Pre-mixed antiquing glaze, dark
   brown

Waterbased polyurethane varnish,
   clear

INSTRUCTIONS

Prepare the Piece:

*Refer to "Preparing the Surface" in
Chapter 2: Creating Textures.*

1. If you are using an old door,
   clean and sand the surface.
   Remove all sanding dust.
2. Prime the surface if it is covered
   with old paint that flakes off.
   Let dry.
3. Basecoat the door with chocolate
   brown latex paint. The dark
   brown will be allowed to show
   through the light colored finish
   on the edges and the thin areas
   of the textured design. Let dry.

Apply Crackle Medium:

Using a brush or roller, apply a
generous coating of crackle
medium to create the aged effect.
Let dry.

Apply Texture Medium:

1. Beginning on the center panel and working your way to the outside,
   spread the texture medium over the door and smooth it with a trowel.
2. Routed trim or sections between the raised panels can make it difficult
   to achieve a smooth application of texture medium. Thin the texture
   medium by stirring a few drops of water into a small amount of the
   texture medium in a disposable container. Apply a heavy layer of
   thinned-down texture medium with a brush to the routed area. Brush
   texture medium over crackle medium with as few strokes of the brush as
   possible, to avoid inhibiting the formation of cracks as the texture
   medium dries.

Add Grid Texture:

1. Lightly mist the grid with water before laying it onto the wet texture
   medium.
2. Spray with a very light mist of water after the grid is in place. This will
   make the process of smoothing the surface much easier. Do not let the
   water puddle. Lightly run the trowel over the grid and the wet texture
   medium.
3. Gently lift the grid off to reveal the impressed grid design.
4. Continue to spread texture medium and impress the grid until the work
   area is covered with the grid design, overlapping the grid into the previous impression to ensure a continuous pattern.

Photo 1. Spraying the grid with water.

Photo 2. Repositioning the grid.

Continued on next page

Pear Orchard Cabinet Door

Continued from page 69

Dry & Sand the Texture:

1. Allow the door to dry overnight.
2. Sand lightly all over to remove rough edges.
3. Sand the texture heavily along parts of the edges and corners to slightly reveal the dark brown base color.

Stencil the Pear Design:

This design has two overlays. Stencil the pears first, let dry, then stencil the leaves.

1. Secure the pear stencil in place with masking tape on the corners.
2. With a thin blade spatula or trowel, apply the texture medium smoothly over the stencil.
3. Carefully peel the stencil back and remove it. Remove excess texture medium from the stencil and rinse it immediately.
4. Allow the raised texture of the pear to dry approximately two hours or until it feels dry. If the texture medium feels cold to the touch, allow it to dry longer until it is room temperature.
5. Using the pear design as your guide, secure the leaf stencil overlay in place, making sure the stencil comes to the edge of the previously applied overlay.
6. With a thin blade spatula or trowel, apply the texture medium smoothly over the stencil.
7. Carefully peel the stencil back and remove it. Remove excess texture medium from the stencil and rinse it immediately.
8. Allow the pear and leaves to dry overnight.

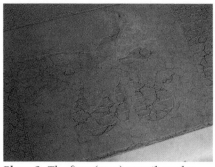

Photo 3. The first (pear) stencil overlay.

Photo 4. Spreading texture medium over the pear stencil.

Photo 5. Removing the pear stencil.

Photo 6. The stenciled pear design.

Photo 7. The second (leaf) stencil overlay.

Photo 8. Spreading texture medium over the leaf stencil.

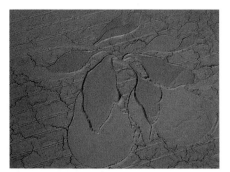

Photo 9. Design when stencils removed.

Apply Paint & Polyurethane:

1. Sand the sharp edges down and smooth the surface all over with a fine sanding block. Use a small piece of sandpaper to smooth small sharp edges or to get into the tight areas.
2. Paint the entire surface with white satin latex or acrylic paint. Allow to dry thoroughly.
3. Apply a coat of polyurethane to create a barrier coat for the next layer. Allow to dry thoroughly.

Antique:

1. Brush on the dark brown glaze.
2. Wipe off the glaze with a soft cloth. This will give the finish a more distressed appearance and accent the textured design.
3. Accentuate the shadows with a round artist's brush and the dark brown glaze. Apply, then brush away excess color. Let dry.
4. Pick up a minute amount of white paint on the tip of a clean, dry chip brush, then wipe it off onto a paper towel. Brush lightly over the entire design. This will highlight the raised areas and give the design even more depth.

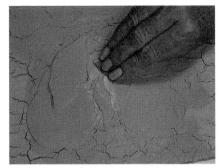

Photo 10. Sanding the pear & leaves design.

Photo 11. Painting with white latex.

Photo 12. Applying dark brown glaze.

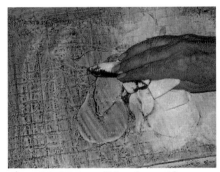

Photo 13. Wiping off the glaze with a cloth.

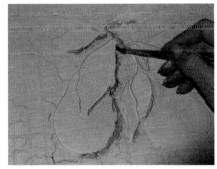

Photo 14. Shading with an artist's brush and dark brown glaze.

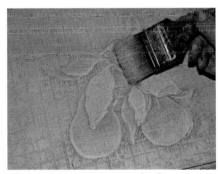

Photo 15. Dry brushing with white paint.

Faux Tiles Backsplash

Create a backsplash in your kitchen with this easy faux tile technique. It can be applied directly on the wall or created on a panel and then attached to the wall.

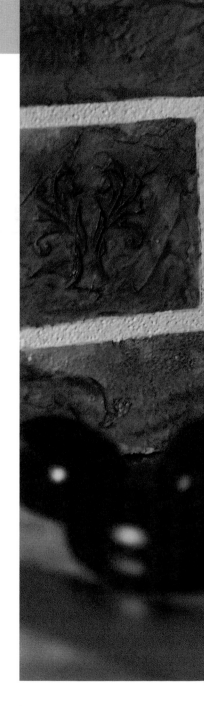

SUPPLIES

Surface:

Hardboard or plywood, size needed for your area

Stencil:

Pre-cut stencil in a fleur-de-lis or floral design

Texture:

Texture medium

Acrylic Paints:

Burnt Sienna

Burnt Umber

Raw Sienna

White – an off-white or antique white shade

Other Tools & Supplies:

Grout tape, ¼" wide, for creating grout lines between tiles

Varnish

INSTRUCTIONS

Preparation:

1. Basecoat the surface with an off-white acrylic paint. Let dry.
2. Measure 1½" in from the top and bottom edges of the surface. Draw horizontal lines with a pencil or chalk pencil.
3. Apply tape inside the lines. The tape will create the look of grout between the tiles.
4. Measure and apply tape in vertical strips to create a row of 5" x 1½" tiles at the top and bottom of the surface.
5. For the center row of tiles, measure and apply tape in vertical strips to create accent tiles that are 2¾" wide alternating with plain tiles that are 1¾" wide.

Apply Texture Medium:

1. Apply texture medium with a palette knife over the entire surface.
2. Before the texture medium dries, carefully remove the tape. Let dry.

Stencil the Accent Tiles:

1. Secure the stencil in place over an accent tile (the wider tiles in the center row).
2. Apply texture medium over the stencil with the palette knife. Carefully peel up the stencil. Remove excess texture from the stencil.
3. Repeat until all accent tiles have the stenciled design. Let dry thoroughly.

Paint the Tiles:

1. Reapply tape to the grout lines.
2. Basecoat the tiles with Raw Sienna acrylic paint. Let dry, leaving the tape in place.

Antique:

1. Mix Burnt Sienna and Burnt Umber acrylic paints for a rich brown color. Thin mixture with water. Apply over the tiles.
2. Wipe back the antiquing with a cloth or paper towel. Let dry.

Finish:

1. Remove the tape from the grout lines.
2. Apply two or more coats of varnish, drying after each coat. ❑

Flourishing Vines Frame

By Kathi Bailey

Frame a friend! This charming square frame is embellished with green and growing vines. It's an easy textured stencil project that gives great results.

SUPPLIES

Surface:
Cardboard frame, 9" x 9"

Stencil:
Vine stencil, cut using the pattern provided

Texture:
Venetian plaster, white

Acrylic Paints:
Burnt Sienna
Vineyard Green

Other Tools & Supplies:
Plastic or foam bowl, for mixing plaster
Stencil brush, for dry brushing
Sandpaper, fine grade, for distressing texture

INSTRUCTIONS

Apply Texture Medium:
1. Pour 1 to 2 cups of plaster into the bowl. Tint the plaster to the desired shade by adding a small amount of Burnt Sienna acrylic paint and stirring to blend thoroughly.
2. Use a putty knife to cover the entire frame with two thin coats of tinted plaster. Let dry after each coat.

Cut the Stencil:
Refer to the stencil cutting instructions at the beginning of this chapter.
1. Photocopy the vine pattern. Enlarge or reduce the pattern if needed.
2. Trace the pattern onto stencil blank material using a fine point marker.
3. Cut out the stencil with a craft knife or stencil burner.

Stencil the Vine Design:
1. Place the stencil on one side of the frame and tape it in place.
2. Apply tinted plaster over the stencil with a putty knife. Carefully peel up the stencil. Remove excess plaster from the stencil.

3. Repeat until all sides of the frame have the stenciled design. Let this first coat of plaster dry for approximately 10 minutes.
4. Repeat the stenciling process on all sides of the frame for a second coat to build up the surface of the design. Let dry completely.

Dry Brush Color:
Pick up a very little Vineyard Green acrylic paint on the tips of the bristles of the stencil brush. Wipe off on a paper towel. Dry brush over the leaves and vines. Let dry.

Finish:
Sand lightly to give a distressed appearance. ❑

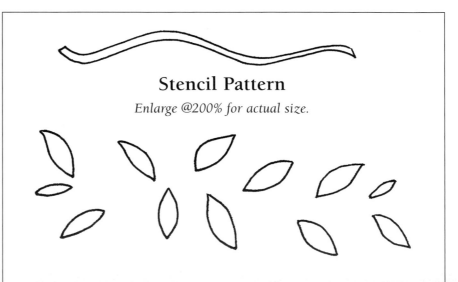

Stencil Pattern
Enlarge @200% for actual size.

Fruitful Abundance Banner

Classical symmetry, subtle colors, crackled surface-this elegant painting looks as if it has an ancient lineage. On this banner, the design is stenciled with acrylic paints, and crackle medium and Venetian plaster produce the antique texture.

SUPPLIES

Surface:
Canvas panel, 28" square

Stencils:
Urn, fruit, and leaf stencils, cut using the patterns provided

Texture:
Venetian plaster, white

Acrylic Paints:
Berry Wine
Burgundy
Hauser Green Dark
Hauser Green Light
Italian Sage
Licorice
Nutmeg
Wicker White
Yellow Ochre

Other Tools & Supplies:
Fabric glue
Crackle medium
Stencil brushes, for applying acrylic paints
Foam plates, for palettes
Natural sponge, for applying antiquing
Sandpaper, 200 grit, for smoothing dried texture
Decorative rod

INSTRUCTIONS

Preparation:
1. Measure and cut the canvas panel to size.
2. Turn under a ½" hem on all sides of canvas. Press to make a crease. Glue the hem down with fabric glue. Tape or put a weight on edges until glue is thoroughly dry.
3. To make a pocket at top for a rod, turn under 2" at the top of the canvas panel (or enough to accommodate the width of your rod). Glue the edge with fabric glue. Let dry thoroughly.
4. Basecoat the canvas with two coats of Nutmeg acrylic paint. Let dry.

Apply Crackle Medium & Topcoat:
1. Apply one coat of crackle medium over the entire panel. Let dry.
2. Apply a second coat of crackle medium to random sections of the canvas. Let dry. This will give a larger crackle effect in those sections.
3. Brush Yellow Ochre over the entire panel. It will crackle as it dries. Let dry thoroughly.

Cut the Stencils:
Refer to the instructions at the beginning of this chapter.
1. Photocopy the patterns. If you enlarge or reduce the patterns, be sure to use the same setting for all the pieces.
2. Trace the patterns onto stencil blank material using a fine point marker.
3. Cut out the stencils with a craft knife or stencil burner.

Stencil the Design:
Follow the same steps to apply color to each piece of the stenciled design.
1. Place the stencil on the banner and tape it in place.
2. Pour a small puddle of paint on a foam plate. Pick up a little paint on a dry stencil brush and pounce up and down on the plate to load the brush. Pounce on a paper towel to remove excess paint. Test on scrap canvas or cardboard to be sure the brush is properly loaded before pouncing through the stencil onto the canvas.
3. Blend colors softly by pouncing over the previously pounced colors.
4. Stencil the parts of the design in this order:
   Urn – Wicker White and Licorice blended to shades of gray. Shade randomly with Nutmeg and Italian Sage.
   Apples – Yellow Ochre, Burgundy, Nutmeg, Wicker White.
   Grapes – Berry Wine, Burgundy, Hauser Green Light, Hauser Green Dark, Nutmeg.

Pears – Yellow Ochre, Hauser Green Light, Burgundy.
Leaves – Hauser Green Light, Hauser Green Dark, Nutmeg, Italian Sage.

Apply Crackle Medium & Texture:
1. Randomly apply crackle medium to areas around the panel and over the edges of the stenciled design. Let dry.

2. With a putty knife, apply Venetian plaster randomly over the crackled areas and other areas of the panel. Let dry.

Antique:
1. Pour a small amount of Nutmeg acrylic paint onto a plate. Thin with 2 to 3 parts water.
2. Dampen the sponge. Dip it into the mixture and wipe over the entire surface to reveal the cracks.
3. Sand the edges to finish.
4. Re-plaster, antique, and sand as desired.

Finish:
Insert the rod and hang the banner.
❏

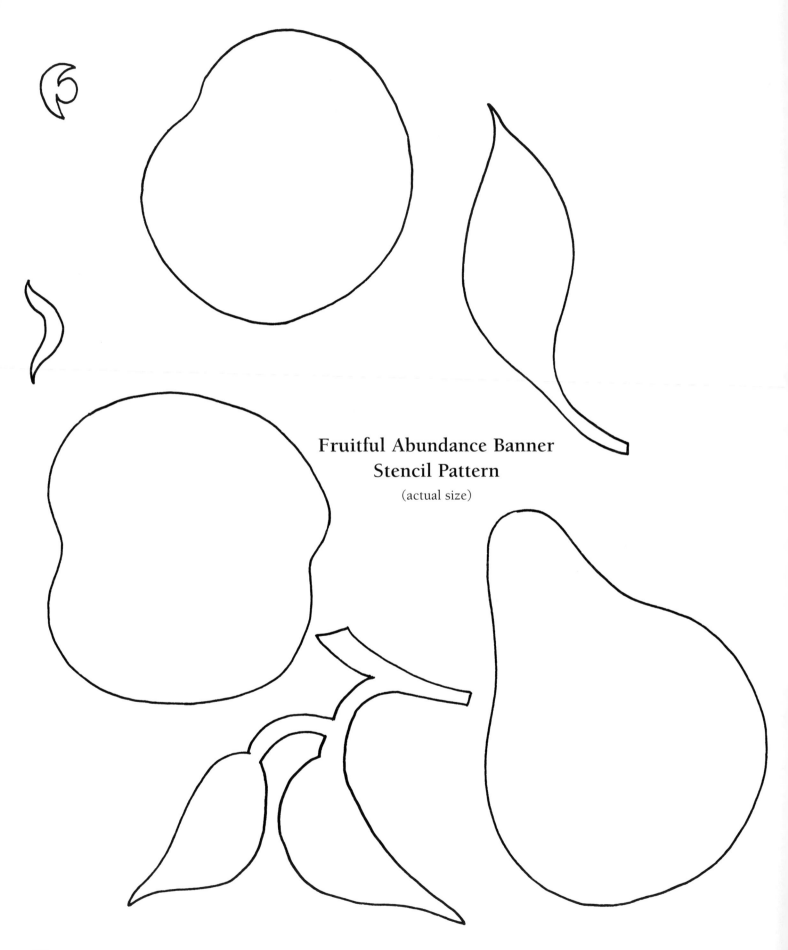

Fruitful Abundance Banner
Stencil Pattern
(actual size)

**Fruitful Abundance Banner
Stencil Pattern**
(actual size)

**Fruitful Abundance Banner
Stencil Pattern**
Enlarge @125% for actual size.

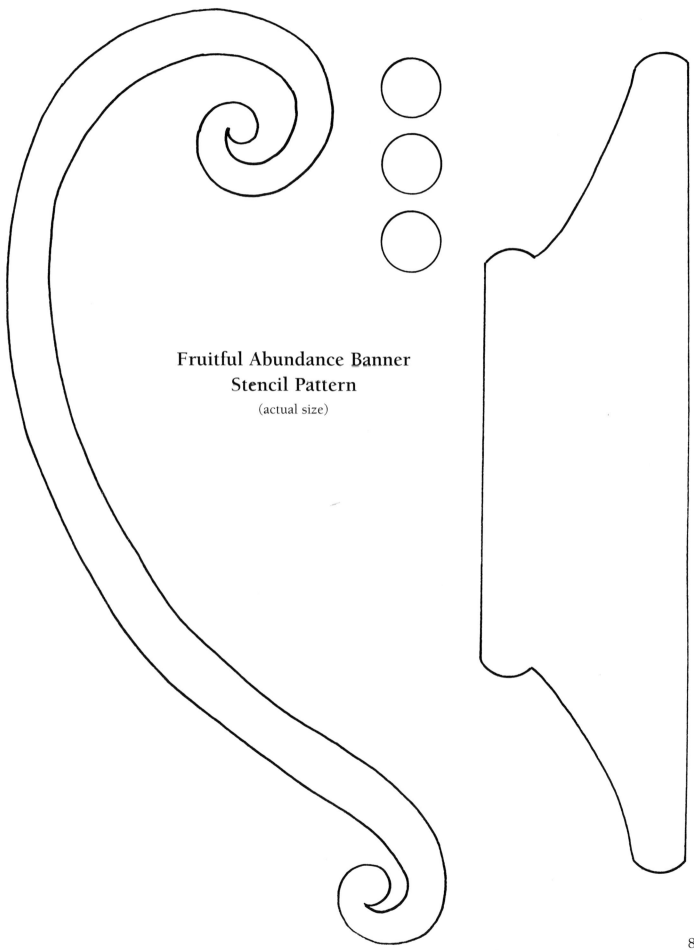

Fruitful Abundance Banner
Stencil Pattern
(actual size)

Classic Marbled Pedestal

What do you want to display? This pedestal can hold an ornamental ceramic vase, a chubby plaster cherub, or a trailing plant with equal poise. The marble effect is created by stirring colorants into the modeling paste just enough to create streaks rather than blending to an even color throughout.

SUPPLIES

Surface:
Wooden pedestal

Stencils:
Pre-cut stencils, architectural ornament designs

Texture:
Modeling paste

Acrylic Paints:
Baby Blue
Deep Midnight Blue
Payne's Gray
Sapphire
Slate Gray

Other Tools & Supplies:
Pearlizing medium
Plastic or foam bowl or plate, for mixing
Artist's fan brush, for dry brushing

INSTRUCTIONS

Preparation:
1. Basecoat the surface with Slate Gray acrylic paint. Let dry.
2. Marbleize the modeling paste. Squeeze out three colors of blue: Baby Blue, Sapphire, and Deep Midnight Blue. Work the color into the modeling paste with a palette knife until you have streaks of blue. Do not over-mix – you want the look of marble.

Stencil the Designs:
1. Apply painter's tape to mask the areas of the stencil that you do not want to use.
2. Place the stencil on one side of the pedestal and tape it in place.
3. Apply marbleized modeling paste over the stencil with the palette knife. Carefully peel up the stencil. Remove excess modeling paste from the stencil. (Photo 1)
4. Repeat until all sides of the pedestal have the stenciled design. Let dry completely.

Antique:
1. Thin Payne's Gray acrylic paint with water. Brush over the surface. (Photo 2)
2. Wipe back with a soft cloth or paper towel. Let dry.

Photo 1. Remove the stencil.

Photo 2. Antique with thinned Payne's Gray.

3. Antique the edges a second time to deepen the color there.
4. Using the artist's fan brush, dry brush pearlizing medium over the edges of the pedestal and the raised areas of the stenciled texture. Let dry. ❑

Lace Filigree Box

If you look at it from a stencil artist's viewpoint, you will conclude that lace is merely an arrangement of open shapes with many bridges. Inexpensive polyester lace holds its shape through the texture stenciling process.

SUPPLIES

Surface:
Wooden box

Stencil:
Lace fabric *(preferably polyester)*

Texture:
Texture medium

Acrylic Paints:
Buttercream
Deep Midnight Blue
Glazing medium

Other Tools & Supplies:
Varnish

INSTRUCTIONS

Preparation:
1. Remove the hinges from the box.
2. Sand the wooden box. Remove sanding dust with a tack cloth.

Stencil the Lace:
Choose a lace that will leave a distinct pattern when used as a stencil. Inexpensive polyester lace is more durable, and holds its shape better when wet.
1. Place the lace fabric over the surface of the box and tape it in place.
2. Apply texture medium over the lace with a palette knife. Carefully peel up the lace. Let the texture medium dry completely.

Paint the Box:
Paint the entire box with Buttercream acrylic paint.

Antique:
1. Thin Deep Midnight Blue acrylic paint with glazing medium. Brush over the surface.
2. Wipe back with a soft cloth or paper towel. Let dry.

Finish:
1. Replace the hinges.
2. Apply two or more coats of varnish, drying after each coat. ❑

Comes the Sun Stepping Stone

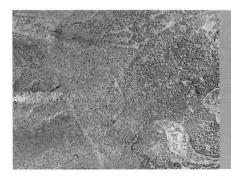

Embellish a stepping stone with a cheerful sun face. This stencil has two overlays-one for the outer shape of the sun, the other for the features of the face-so it doesn't require many bridges that could make the design confusing.

SUPPLIES

Surface:

Concrete stepping stone, available at garden centers and home improvement stores

Stencil:

Sun stencil, two overlays, cut from the patterns in this book

Texture:

Sand texture medium

Acrylic Paints:

Charcoal Gray

Driftwood

Warm White

Yellow Oxide

Other Tools & Supplies:

Artist's fan brush, for dry brushing

INSTRUCTIONS

Cut the Stencils:

Refer to the instructions at the beginning of this chapter.

1. Use a photocopier to enlarge the patterns if needed. Be sure to enlarge the sun shape pattern and the facial features pattern at the same setting.
2. Cut out the stencils with a craft knife or stencil burner.

Stencil the Design:

1. Place the sun shape stencil on the stepping stone and tape it in place.
2. Apply texture medium over the stencil with a palette knife. Carefully peel up the stencil. Let dry.
3. Center the facial features stencil on the sun shape and tape it in place.
4. Apply texture medium over the stencil with the palette knife. Carefully peel up the stencil. Let dry.

Antique:

1. Thin Charcoal Gray acrylic paint with water. Brush over the surface.
2. Wipe back with a soft cloth or paper towel. Let dry.
3. Dry brush with Driftwood acrylic paint.
4. Dry brush with Yellow Oxide, then Warm White acrylic paint. ❑

Comes the Sun Stepping Stone
Stencil Pattern

Enlarge to fit the size of your stone.

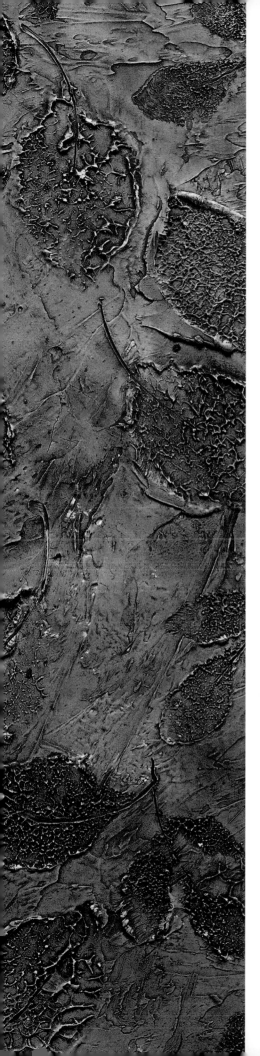

CHAPTER 5

Creating Texture with Embossing

Almost anything can be pressed into wet texture medium to leave its pattern when the texture dries. Leaves and other natural objects, gears and other machine parts, metal grates and grids, crumpled plastic bags from the dry cleaner, rubber pads for skid-proofing rugs-the list is limited only by your imagination and readiness to experiment.

Rubber and foam stamps are made for creating impressions. There are many stamps on the market that you can use with texture medium. Look for foam or rubber stamps that have large flat areas. A stamp with a lot of detail will not create a firm impression in the texture medium. Rinse stamps immediately after use; they will be ruined if texture medium dries in the stamp.

If you don't find a design you like, you can design and carve your own stamps. The instructions are all in this chapter.

SUPPLIES

RUBBER AND FOAM STAMPS

Craft stores and home decor centers are good sources for stamps in many designs. Choose stamps without a lot of detail. Some stamp manufacturers produce stamps that are designed to be used for stamping on walls; they have large flat areas and distinctive silhouettes that make them a good choice for stamping into texture medium.

TOOLS & SUPPLIES FOR DESIGNING AND CARVING STAMPS

Styrofoam or rubber blocks: Use a material that is easy to carve. You can even cut stamps out of a potato if you like. Craft stores sell blocks of carving material for making your own stamps.

Craft knife: Use a knife with replaceable blades, and keep plenty of extra blades on hand.

Self-healing cutting mat: Use for protecting your work surface from craft knife cuts and prolonging the life of your blades.

Tracing paper, markers, pencils, etc.: Drawing papers and tools for working out your designs.

Transfer paper: Transfer paper has a graphite coating on one side. Place it between a tracing of your design and the surface. With a stylus or ballpoint pen, trace over the lines of the design with just enough pressure to transfer the lines to the surface.

TEXTURE, ANTIQUING, AND FINISHING SUPPLIES

Texture Medium: For best results when doing decoupage combined with texture medium, use a medium that has a fine to medium texture and that is not thick. *See the discussion of "Texture Products" in the General Supplies chapter.*

Tools for Applying Texture:
- Palette knife, metal or plastic blade
- Putty knife
- Trowel

See the discussion of tools needed in the "Texturing Tools" section of the General Supplies chapter.

Paints:
Use acrylic paints for basecoating surfaces, adding color to areas of a project, and coloring glazes and antiquing mixtures.

Finishes:
Use a waterbased varnish for protecting dried, completed projects.

OTHER TOOLS & SUPPLIES

In addition to the tools and supplies you use for preparing the surface, applying texture, antiquing, and finishing, you will need:

- Chip brush, for applying antiquing mixtures and glazes
- Foam brush, for applying paints, mediums, and finishes
- Artist's brushes, for painting details
- Palette knife or wooden stirring sticks, for stirring
- Palette, or plastic or foam plates or trays, for setting out and mixing mediums and paints
- Paper shop towels or clean cloths, for wiping glazes and antiquing
- Painter's tape, for masking
- Metal ruler, for measuring
- Pencil or fine point marker, for marking, tracing or drawing
- Scissors or craft knife, for cutting paper, cardboard, fabric, or plastic
- Self-healing cutting mat, for protecting your work surface from craft knife cuts
- Sandpaper, in various grades, for preparing surfaces and smoothing dried texture
- Tack cloth, for removing sanding dust
- Water containers, for rinsing brushes and thinning paints
- Damp cloth or baby wipes, for cleaning your hands, tools or surfaces
- Dishpan filled with water, for holding tools until you can clean them
- Plastic tablecloth, for protecting your work area

BASIC INSTRUCTIONS

MAKING YOUR OWN STAMPS

If you don't find a ready-made stamp you like, you can create your own by carving a design into a block of plastic foam, a piece of rubber, or even a potato. You can purchase linoleum or plastic blocks especially made for carving stamps at art and craft stores. You can also create stamps from craft foam by gluing several layers together to get the depth of stamp that you want. Ideas for stamp designs can come from your own drawings or from a number of copyright-free publications or on-line sources. You can use your computer to make designs with words and lettering. Look for shapes you like in nature; leaves can be the basis for your design. Geometric shapes and large letters are easy to cut and will make good models for stamps. When you are designing a stamp, remember that the image will be reversed when the stamp is applied to the surface. This is especially important if your design includes letters. Check your design by looking at it in a mirror before you begin to carve your stamp.

Carving a Stamp

1. Trace your design onto tracing paper and tape the tracing onto the stamp material.
2. Rub the back of the design with a soft pencil, place the tracing paper on the stamp material, and draw over the design lines just firmly enough to transfer the design to the stamp material. (You could also use transfer paper.) Be careful not to impress lines into the stamp material. If your design is large and simple, tape the tracing to the stamp material.
3. Cut out the area that is not part of the design with a craft knife with a new, sharp blade. Draw the knife around the outside edge of the design, slicing down into the material, then make horizontal cuts from the outside edge of the material to the vertical cut, so you can lift out a layer of material.
4. Continue until you have carved out the area that is not part of the design.

EMBOSSING THE TEXTURE MEDIUM

Stamping into wet texture medium impresses your design into the surface.

Here's how:

1. Apply the texture medium using a palette knife, or use any of the other tools and techniques. Make a layer of texture medium about the same depth as your stamp relief.
2. Smooth the surface for smaller stamps so as not to compete with the impressed design.
3. Use a thicker texture medium, or allow the texture medium to set up a bit before pressing the stamp.
4. Press the stamp straight down onto the surface and rock the stamp back and forth a bit. This will push the texture medium out from under the area of the stamp.
5. Repeat to create more impressions, wiping the stamp clean with a paper towel after each use.
6. If there is an area you are not happy with, smooth the texture with the palette knife and try again.

Stamp carved from a plastic foam block.

Stamping into wet texture medium.

Embossed Foliage Tray

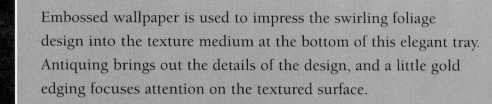

Embossed wallpaper is used to impress the swirling foliage design into the texture medium at the bottom of this elegant tray. Antiquing brings out the details of the design, and a little gold edging focuses attention on the textured surface.

SUPPLIES

Surface:

Wooden tray

Embossing Material:

Textured wallpaper with an embossed leaf and floral design

Texture:

Texture medium

Acrylic Paints:

Burgundy

Gold

Glazing medium

Other Tools & Supplies:

Artist's fan brush, for dry brushing

Varnish

Textured wallpaper used on the tray.

INSTRUCTIONS

Preparation:

1. Cut a piece of wallpaper that is larger than the area you wish to cover.
2. Using a palette knife, apply texture medium to the surface of the tray.

Impress the Design:

1. Press the wallpaper into the texture. Be sure to press evenly over the entire area.
2. Carefully peel up the wallpaper.
3. Let the texture dry thoroughly.

Antique:

1. Thin Burgundy acrylic paint with glazing medium. Apply to the textured surface with a chip brush.
2. Wipe back with a soft cloth or paper towel. Let dry.

Finish:

1. Paint the edges and back of the tray with Burgundy acrylic paint.
2. Brush Gold acrylic paint on the border. Wipe with a paper towel to remove excess and allow a little of the Burgundy to show.
3. Dry brush Gold acrylic paint over the textured area.
4. Apply two or more coats of varnish, drying after each coat. ❑

Rose Tea Box

By Rose Wilde

This tea box is resurfaced with Rose Wilde's "Cracklin' Rose" signature design, using her rubber stamp in an all-over pattern. You could also use other flower stamps with distinctive silhouettes or a paisley shaped stamp.

SUPPLIES

Surface:

Wooden box

Embossing Implement:

Rose stamp

Texture:

Texture medium

Paint:

Latex paint for basecoating, dark chocolate brown

Other Tools & Supplies:

Crackle medium

Sandpaper, for preparing the surface

Spray bottle, filled with water for misting surfaces

Antiquing stain, dark brown.

Polyurethane varnish, waterbased or solvent based

Before

INSTRUCTIONS

Preparation:

Gather some paint cans or plastic items that will fit inside the lid and the box and act as supports to keep the wet surfaces elevated until they dry. (Turn the box upside down on the support.)

1. Sand the box lightly. Remove all traces of sanding dust with a tack cloth.
2. Basecoat with dark chocolate brown. Let dry.

Apply Crackle Medium:

Brush crackle medium over the box and lid. Let dry.

Stamp the Design:

1. Spread texture medium evenly over the lid.
2. Lightly mist the surface, then immediately press in the dampened rose stamp. Let dry.
3. Spread texture medium evenly over the box.

Continued on page 96

Top of box

Photo 1. Applying the basecoat.

Photo 2. Applying crackle medium.

Photo 3. Spreading texture medium evenly.

Photo 4. Covering the lid with texture medium.

95

Rose Tea Box

Continued from page 95

4. Lightly mist the surface, then immediately press in the dampened rose stamp. You may only be able to apply parts of the rose stamp to the smaller sections of the box, which will give the illusion of an all-over rose design.

5. Set aside the lid and box to dry overnight, elevated on their supports.

6. Rinse stamps and tools immediately.

Finish:

1. As the texture dries, cracks will appear. Once dry, sand to remove rough areas.

2. Apply stain in liberal amounts, being sure to fill all the cracks and crevasses.

3. Wipe away the excess stain with a shop towel or cloth. Let dry.

4. Apply a coat of varnish. ❏

Photo 5. Misting the surface.

Photo 6. Pressing in the dampened stamp.

Photo 7. Lifting off the stamp.

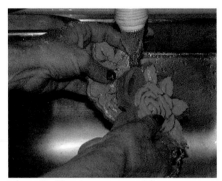

Photo 8. Cleaning stamps with water.

Photo 9. Staining the crackled texture.

Photo 10. Dry brushing to highlight the texture.

Rose Stool

By Rose Wilde
The same techniques used on the Rose Tea Box were used to decorate this charming little stool, assembled from odds and ends of flea market finds. The top is cushioned with an embossed rose fabric. You can easily adapt the techniques to create a small stool or box of your own.

Cork Finish Cabinet Door

By Rose Wilde
This richly detailed surface is created with a crumpled plastic bag pressed into wet texture medium. Glazing brings out all the variations in texture.

SUPPLIES

Surface:

Cabinet door

Embossing Material:

Plastic wrap

Texture:

Texture medium

Paint:

Black acrylic paint

Other Tools & Supplies:

Clear plastic laminate with peel-off backing, for the tree mask

Permanent black marker, for the tree mask

Antiquing glaze, golden brown

Polyurethane varnish, waterbased or solvent based

INSTRUCTIONS

Preparation:

Sand the surface of the door lightly if needed. Remove sanding dust with a tack cloth.

Tree Silhouette Mask:

1. Draw a silhouette of a tree with a black marker onto the clear laminate use the pattern provided, enlarging to size needed for your door.
2. Peel off the backing and adhere the laminate to the center panel of the cabinet door.
3. Cut around the tree silhouette with a craft knife. Remove the blank areas of the laminate, leaving only the black design on the panel.

Apply Texture Medium:

Apply a thick layer of texture medium over the entire silhouette. Smooth with a thin blade trowel, being careful not to disturb the tree mask underneath.

Impress the Texture:

1. Crumple a dry, thin plastic bag. Lay it over the texture medium. Smooth and press gently with your hands, so the plastic bag impresses all of the wet texture surface.
2. Carefully lift the plastic bag straight up and off, leaving peaks and wrinkles behind.
3. Immediately peel the tree mask up and off, removing the texture medium from the tree silhouette.
4. Allow the texture medium to dry overnight to a hard, crisp surface.

Photo 1. Adhering the tree silhouette mask.

Photo 2. Applying texture medium.

Photo 3. Pressing the crumpled plastic bag into the texture medium.

Photo 4. Lifting off the plastic bag.

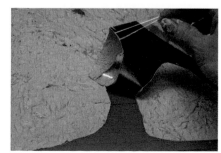

Photo 5. Removing the mask.

Continued on next page

Cork Finish Cabinet Door

Continued from page 99

Glaze & Paint the Door:

1. Sand the surface until it is as smooth as possible without removing all the texture and pits that were formed with the crumpled plastic bag. Remove all traces of sanding dust.
2. Apply a liberal amount of golden brown glaze or stain, being careful to fill all the cracks and crevices with the stain.
3. Wipe off the excess, making the top surface a lighter color and leaving darker color in the grooves and pits in order to accent the textured design.
4. Using a small artist's brush, paint the silhouette design black.
5. Allow to dry thoroughly.

Finish:

Apply three coats of varnish to ensure a durable finish, drying after each coat. Waterbased or solvent-based polyurethane are both acceptable for a protective coating. ❏

Photo 6. Applying the glaze.

Photo 7. Wiping back the glaze.

Photo 8. Painting the tree silhouette.

Cork Finish Cabinet Door
Tree Pattern

Western Trunk

By Rose Wilde

This trunk was purchased at a flea market for only $30. It was transformed from trash to treasure with texture, crackle effects, paint, and stain. No stripping required!

Western Trunk before

Close-up of the top of the trunk

The tooled leather design on the top of the trunk is made by pressing lace into wet texture medium. Crackle medium produces the cracked wood appearance on the slat boards. Apply a coat of crackle medium, let it dry, then apply a smooth coat of texture medium; cracks form as the texture dries.

To create the aged leather look on the bottom half of the trunk, apply a smooth coat of texture medium, then press a wet t-shirt into the wet texture medium. When you lift off the shirt, it leaves wrinkles on the surface.

Once it is completely dry (overnight) and sanded over, stain the entire surface with a water-based golden brown stain. Wipe back the stain with a soft cloth, making the surface lighter and leaving darker stain in the wrinkles and impressed lace texture.

The ornamental metal trim pieces are painted with gold metallic paint. When the gold paint dries, brush on a verdigris patina to enhance the weathered charm of the trunk.

Fallen Leaves Table

The stamped design on this small tabletop was inspired by Nature's infinite variety of leaf shapes and sizes. The leaf shapes are so easy to carve that you can quickly make six of them on a single cube of plastic foam.

SUPPLIES

Surface:
Wooden tabletop

Embossing Implements:
Carved leaf stamps

Texture:
Texture medium

Acrylic Paint:
Burnt Umber
Glazing medium

Other Tools & Supplies:
Plastic foam block, for carving stamps
Polyurethane varnish, waterbased or solvent based

Pictured above: Top of table

Pictured at left: A stamp carved from plastic foam.

Instructions begin on page 106.

FALLEN LEAVES TABLE

Continued from page 104

INSTRUCTIONS

Carve the Stamps:

1. Trace the leaf patterns from this book and transfer the designs onto the plastic foam block.
2. Carve around the designs with a craft knife.

Apply Texture Medium:

Apply a layer of texture medium over the tabletop, about the same depth as the stamp relief.

Impress the Stamps:

1. Press the stamp evenly into the texture medium. Wipe the stamp and press as often as necessary to cover the tabletop. Use several of each of the leaf sizes.
2. Add stems and veins with the edge of the palette knife. Draw the knife through the texture and wipe off the excess medium from the blade.
3. Rinse stamps and tools immediately.
4. Allow the texture to dry overnight.

Antique:

1. Thin Burnt Umber acrylic paint with extender medium. Apply with a chip brush. You may use wood stain or premixed glaze instead of the paint.
2. Wipe back with a soft cloth or paper towel. Let dry.

Finish:

Apply two or more coats of varnish, drying after each coat. ❑

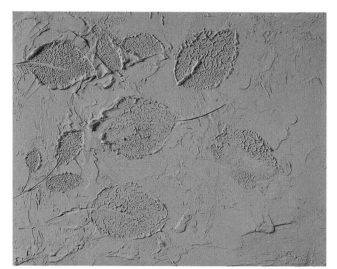

The design stamped into the texture medium

The texture piece after antiquing

Pattern for Stamps

(actual size)

CHAPTER 6

Fun & Easy Techniques

This chapter introduces some techniques and projects that will get your imagination in gear.

Mosaics have become popular for decorating containers, tabletops, stepping stones, and other surfaces. Two of the projects in this chapter create mosaic effects with texture medium: one embeds sparkling bits of sea glass in the texture; the other is a faux mosaic made by drawing grout lines into wet texture medium with the tip of a palette knife.

If you enjoy decorative painting, you will be pleased to find that the dried texture makes an excellent surface for painting with acrylic paints. Decorative painting designs can join your growing collection of texture medium possibilities.

SUPPLIES

OBJECTS FOR EMBEDDING

Small decorative items can be embedded into the texture medium to create a mosaic look. Here are some interesting items that can be used to embed:
- Sea glass
- Ceramic pieces
- Glass or ceramic mosaic tiles
- Shells, pebbles, faux gems, etc.

TEXTURE, ANTIQUING, AND FINISHING SUPPLIES

Texture Medium: For best results when doing decoupage combined with texture medium, use a medium that has a fine to medium texture and that is not thick. *See the discussion of "Texture Products" in the General Supplies chapter.*

Tools for Applying Texture:
- Palette knife, metal or plastic blade
- Putty knife
- Trowel

See the discussion of tools needed in the "Texturing Tools" section of the General Supplies chapter.

Paints:
Use acrylic paints for basecoating surfaces, adding color to areas of a project, and coloring glazes and antiquing mixtures.

Finishes:
Use a waterbased varnish for protecting dried, completed projects.

SUPPLIES FOR DECORATIVE PAINTING

Bottled craft acrylics are perfect for painting on textured surfaces. They come in an array of colors, dry quickly, and clean up easily with soap and water.

Palette: You will need a palette for laying out and mixing paints. Foam plates or deli packaging trays work well. Move and mix paints with a clean palette knife.

Brushes: You need only a few artist's brushes to paint the designs in this section of the book: a 1" flat for basecoating, a #6 round for most of the painting, and a liner for details and outlines. Keep a brush basin with two water wells (or small plastic tubs filled with water) on your worktable, one side for rinsing brushes and the other with clean water for thinning paints. Rinse your brushes as soon as you finish an area of color; never let paint dry in the brush. Wash your brushes with mild soap and water when you finish your painting session.

OTHER TOOLS & SUPPLIES

In addition to the tools and supplies you use for preparing the surface, applying texture, antiquing, and finishing, you will need:

- Chip brush, for applying antiquing mixtures and glazes
- Foam brush, for applying paints, mediums, and finishes
- Artist's brushes, for painting details
- Palette knife or wooden stirring sticks, for stirring
- Palette, or plastic or foam plates or trays, for setting out and mixing mediums and paints
- Paper shop towels or clean cloths, for wiping glazes and antiquing
- Painter's tape, for masking
- Metal ruler, for measuring
- Pencil, chalk pencil, and fine point marker, for marking, tracing or drawing
- Scissors or craft knife, for cutting paper, cardboard, fabric, or plastic
- Self-healing cutting mat, for protecting your work surface from craft knife cuts
- Sandpaper, in various grades, for preparing surfaces and smoothing dried texture
- Tack cloth, for removing sanding dust
- Water containers, for rinsing brushes and thinning paints
- Damp cloth or baby wipes, for cleaning your hands, tools or surfaces
- Dishpan filled with water, for holding tools until you can clean them
- Plastic tablecloth, for protecting your work area

BASIC INSTRUCTIONS

EMBEDDING OBJECTS INTO TEXTURE MEDIUM

Sea glass, mosaic tiles, bits of broken china, even small toys-embedding objects into the texture medium is easy.

1. Lay out the objects on the surface and move them around until you have an arrangement you like. Draw a placement diagram on a sheet of paper for reference when you begin placing the objects in the wet texture.
2. Remove the objects from the surface and place them where you can reach them easily as you work.
3. Mix colorants into the texture medium if you like.
4. Cover your surface with a generous amount of texture medium so there is enough material to hold the embedded object. (If it comes loose later, don't worry—you can always glue it back in place.)
5. Press the objects into the wet texture medium with your fingers. Press hard enough to embed the object without covering the surface of the object. Wipe your hands on paper towels or baby wipes to avoid leaving unwanted texture on the surfaces of the objects you are embedding.
6. Since you use a thicker layer of texture for this technique, your project will take a bit longer to dry. Allow for extra curing time.

PAINTING TEXTURED SURFACES

Use the same decorative painting techniques and materials for painting on textured surfaces as you use on wood or other surfaces. There are many books and classes that teach decorative painting, and many designs that are available.

TIPS:

Using a Liner brush: Thin paint with water or extender medium to the consistency of ink. Load the liner by pulling it through the puddle of paint as you twirl it to form a point. Hold it with the brush handle pointing straight up, touch the tip of the liner to the surface, and pull the stroke using your arm and shoulder, not your wrist alone. You can steady your stroke by moving your extended little finger along the surface.

Thinning acrylic paints: Thin acrylics with water or extender medium. The extender medium gives you a longer open time to blend colors before the paint dries.

Transferring patterns: All the patterns are included with the instructions for individual projects. Enlarge and reduce the patterns on a photocopier if necessary. To transfer the pattern to the surface, you will need tracing paper, graphite transfer paper, and a stylus. Use gray transfer paper on light-colored surfaces, and light gray or white transfer paper on dark-colored surfaces.

1. Trace the design.
2. Tape the tracing paper in place on the project surface.
3. Slide the transfer paper under the tracing paper.
4. Draw over the pattern lines with a stylus.
5. Before you remove the tape, lift the tracing and transfer papers to be sure all the pattern lines have transferred.
6. If any lines are showing after the paint dries, gently remove them with a kneaded eraser.

Embedded Sea Glass Tray

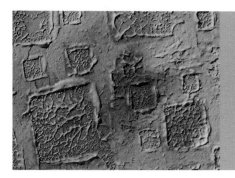

Texture, stamped impressions, and sea glass give this squared-off tray a lot of tactile interest. Lay out a pattern with the stamps and bits of glass, or place them spontaneously-it all works.

SUPPLIES

Surface:

Wooden plate

Objects for Embedding:

Sea glass pieces, clear and blue-green

Embossing Implements:

Square stamps in various sizes (or carve your own stamp using a plastic foam block)

Texture:

Texture medium

Acrylic Paints:

Raw Sienna

Teal Green

Glazing medium

Other Tools & Supplies:

Plastic foam block, for carving stamps

Varnish

INSTRUCTIONS

Apply Texture Medium:

Apply texture medium to the center of the plate.

Impress the Stamps:

Press the stamp evenly into the texture medium. Wipe the stamp and press as often as necessary to cover the area. Use several of each size square.

Embed the Sea Glass:

Choose flat pieces to maximize the contact area with the texture.

1. Apply texture medium thickly to the wide rim of the plate.
2. With your fingers, press the sea glass pieces into the texture. You can create a pattern or just apply them randomly.
3. Let dry overnight.

Antique:

1. Thin Raw Sienna acrylic paint with glazing medium. Apply with a chip brush to the center of the plate.
2. Wipe back with a soft cloth or paper towel.
3. Apply the antiquing around the glass pieces on the rim of the plate.
4. Wipe back with a soft cloth or paper towel.
5. Wipe excess antiquing from the glass with a damp paper towel. Let dry thoroughly.

Finish:

1. Paint the back of the plate with Teal Green acrylic paint. Let dry.
2. Apply two or more coats of varnish to the plate, drying after each coat. ❑

Painted Roses Box

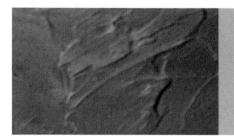

Sweetly feminine, this ring-around-the-rosie box is a lovely addition to a dressing table or powder room.

SUPPLIES

Surface:
Round wooden box

Texture:
Texture medium, fine texture

Acrylic Paints:
Burgundy
Burnt Umber
Buttermilk
Pine Green
Raw Sienna
Ultramarine Blue

Artist's Brushes:
1" flat for basecoating
#6 round
#0 liner

Other Tools & Supplies:
Tracing paper, for tracing patterns
Transfer paper and stylus, for trans-
    ferring patterns to the surface
Toothbrush, for spattering
Varnish

INSTRUCTIONS

Apply Texture Medium:
Apply texture medium to the box with a palette knife. Leave the lid on the box and apply the texture on the sides up to the lid so the sides will not become too thick for the lid to fit on the box. Let dry.

Basecoat the Box:
Basecoat the box and lid with Buttermilk acrylic paint. Let dry.

Transfer the Design:
1. Trace the design.
2. Tape the tracing paper in place on the box. Slide the transfer paper under the tracing paper. Draw over the pattern lines with a stylus.

Continued on page 114

Painted Roses Box

Continued from page 112

3. Measure from the bottom edge of the box and mark at ½" and 1". With a pencil or chalk pencil, draw two lines around the box to define the edges of the green stripe.

Paint the Design:

Thin the paints with clean water. If you want more open time for painting, thin the paints with extender medium instead.

1. Using the #6 round artist's brush and thinned paint, fill in the first layer of the painting:
   Circles for the rose shapes – Burgundy
   Leaves – Pine Green
   Swags – Raw Sienna
2. Add the second layer of paint, again thinned with water:
   Bottoms and centers of roses – Burgundy
   Stem ends and sides of leaves – Pine Green
   Under the traced lines of the swags – Burnt Umber
3. Add line work around the edges of all the elements. Use the liner brush and thin the paint to the consistency of ink.
   Around roses – a mixture of Burgundy + Burnt Umber
   Around leaves – a mixture of Pine Green + Burnt Umber
   Around swags – Burnt Umber

Paint the Trim:

1. Paint the band around the top of the box with a wash of thinned Burgundy.
2. Paint a line around the inside edge of the Burnt Umber on the swags.
3. Wash the stripe around the bottom of the box with a thinned mixture of Pine Green + Burgundy.
4. Paint a line on either side of the stripe with a mixture of Burnt Umber + Raw Sienna.
5. Allow the paint to dry thoroughly.

Antique:

1. Thin Raw Sienna acrylic paint with water. Apply to the entire surface of the box and lid.
2. Wipe back with a soft cloth or paper towel. Let dry.
3. Repeat the antiquing with Burnt Umber, then Ultramarine Blue.
4. To spatter, thin Burnt Umber with water to the consistency of ink. Dip the toothbrush bristles into the puddle of paint. Holding the toothbrush above

PAINT THE DESIGN

Step 1. First layer of paint.

Step 2. Second layer of paint.

Step 3. Linework painted.

Design painted on the side of the box.

and to the side of the box, bristles pointing down, pull your thumb across the bristles back toward your body to release a spatter of droplets. You may also use a wooden stirring stick or the edge of a palette knife. Practice on scrap paper or cardboard until you achieve an effect you like, then spatter the box. Let dry.

5. With a paper towel, buff the texture to remove some of the antiquing from the tops of the texture.

Finish:
Apply two or more coats of varnish, drying after each coat. ❏

Pattern for Side of Box

(actual size)

Painted Roses Box
Pattern for Top of Box
(actual size)

CHAPTER 7

Using Napkins for Decoupage

Napkins are great for decoupage since they are thinner than the other papers and almost become absorbed into the surface. This makes them great for applying over a textured surface because they form themselves over the underlying texture. The napkin design will appear as a painted design on the textured surface.

Antiquities Framed Canvas

This project combines all of the techniques we have used painting, stenciling and decoupage. Short of doing a fresco on your walls, creating a large canvas to frame or hang is a way to get the look into your décor.

SUPPLIES

Surface:
Canvas board, 18" x 24"
Frame of your choice

Paper:
Napkins in neoclassical style
Paper for background with an over-all neoclassical pattern such as scrapbook paper, two styles
Additional papers of your choice

Texture:
Texture medium

Acrylic Paints:
Raw Umber
Light Parchment
Black
Extender
Glazing medium

Other Tools & Supplies:
Decoupage medium
Varnish (optional)
Stencils with architectural motifs
Masking Tape
Chip brush to apply antiquing
Sponge brush for glue
Artist brushes, 1" flat wash, #6 filbert, fan brush
Plastic foam tray
Stylus
Tracing Paper
Transfer Paper
Scissors
Palette knife

INSTRUCTIONS

Decoupage background:
1. Tear sheets of the background paper into large pieces.
2. Attach the pieces of the background paper to the canvas board using decoupage medium. Cover entire canvas with the pieces of paper.

Apply Texture Medium:
Apply texture medium here and there over the background. Allow to dry. *(Photo 1)*

Paint the Design:
See Painting Worksheet for step by step of painting the design.
1. Trace design for urn. Transfer the design to the surface.
2. Wash entire design area with Raw Umber.
3. Dip the large wash brush in extender and blot on paper towel. Side-load Raw Umber into one side of brush. Shade the right side of urn.
4. Shade under each of the horizontal lines.
5. Shade on the left side of the urn but to a lesser amount.
6. Shade between the raised ovals shade and on both sides of the handles.
7. Dry brush the highlight with Light Parchment using the fan brush.
8. Deepen the shading with Black on the right side of the urn, above the scallops, above and below the horizontal sections, the right sides of the handles, and to the right of the of the raised design area.
9. Dry brush highlight with Light Parchment. Allow painting to dry. *(Photo 2)*

Decoupage:
Using images from napkins and other images of your choice, apply these images randomly with decoupage medium, — some on top of the painting. Let dry.

Apply Texture Medium:
1. Using the stencil, apply texture medium through the stencil in various places on canvas. Use photo as an example.
2. Apply additional texture medium over some areas of the painting. Let dry.

Finish:
1. Antique the entire canvas with Raw Umber that is mixed with glazing medium to make an antiquing glaze.
2. Dry brush raised areas of the texture with Light Parchment.
3. Apply varnish. Let dry. ❑

Photo 1

Photo 2

Antiquities Framed Canvas
Pattern

Enlarge at 200% for actual size
See photo on page 119
See instructions on page 118

Antiquities Framed Canvas Painting Worksheet

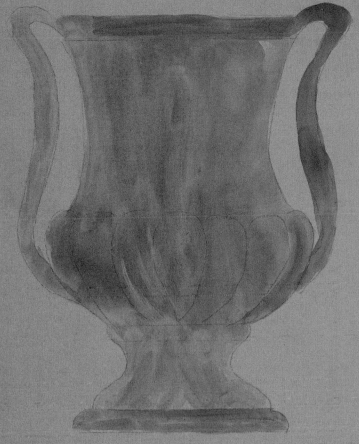

Wash with Raw Umber

Shade using wash brush
sideloaded with Raw Umber

Drybrush highlights

Deepen Shading

Canvas Triptych

This project uses a combination of different types of papers in a collage. Combining items with a similar color range or theme works best. Look for a larger central image and then portions of images for the other parts of the collage. The central images that I used were urns of flowers from napkins for two of the canvases, and a classical scene from decoupage paper for the third canvas.

SUPPLIES

Surface:
Three 11" x 14" pre-stretched
   canvases
4 hinges

Paper:
Napkins of your choice
   (pictured above)
Decoupage paper
Assorted collage papers

Texture:
Texture Medium

Acrylic Paint:
Burnt Umber
Buttermilk
Glazing medium

Other Tools & Supplies:
Decoupage medium
Sponge brush for applying glue
Chip brush for applying antiquing
Artist's fan brush for dry brushing
Scissors
Palette knife
Varnish

INSTRUCTIONS

Preparation:
Apply texture medium to the entire front and side surface of each of the canvases with a palette knife. Let dry.

Decoupage:
1. Arrange your chosen images on the canvas and play with the overlapping and positioning until the composition pleases you. If you are using very thin papers such as napkins, the paper underneath will show

Photo 1

Photo 2

Photo 3

Photo 4

through creating more interesting effects. *(Photo 1)*

2. Attach the papers to the canvases using decoupage medium. Let dry. *(Photo 2)*

Texture:
Add additional texture medium on top of the collage in random areas. Let dry. *(Photos 3 & 4)*

Finish:
1. Mix the Burnt Umber paint with the glazing medium to create a thin antiquing glaze. Antique the entire surface of each of the canvases with Burnt Umber. Let dry.
2. Dry brush areas of the collage with Buttermilk acrylic paint. Let dry.
3. Varnish the three canvases.
4. Hinge the canvases together. ❑

Butterfly Frame

This wide wooden frame was covered with one single napkin. The napkin I used was larger that the frame and had a border. I cut the border from the one side and glued that first then trimmed the rest of the napkin to fit, fitting the border along the edge of frame.

SUPPLIES

Surface:
Wide wooden frame, 11" x 12-1/2"

Paper:
Napkin large enough to cover frame

Texture:
Texture Medium

Acrylic Paint:
Buttermilk
Blue or color to match your napkin

Other Tools & Supplies:
Decoupage medium
Chip brush for applying antiquing
Artist's fan brush for dry brushing
Sponge brush for applying glue
Scissors
Palette knife
Varnish

INSTRUCTIONS

Preparation:
1. Paint the side edges of the frame blue or color of your choice. Let dry.
2. Apply texture medium to the entire front surface of the frame. Let dry.

Decoupage:
1. Cut your napkin to fit the frame. If your napkin has a border like mine did, cut off the border pieces to fit the frame. *(Photo 1)*
2. Attach the napkin to the surface using decoupage medium. Spread the medium on the surface and then place the napkin. Cut an ìXî in the center section of the napkin where the napkin is over frame opening. Spread decoupage medium onto the inside edge of the frame opening and the back of the frame. Bring napkin to back of frame in the center opening area. Let dry. *(Photo 2)*

Finish:
1. Dry brush the high areas of the textured piece with Buttermilk paint using fan brush. Let dry. *(Photo 3)*
2. Varnish. ❑

Photo 1

Photo 2

Photo 3

METRIC CONVERSION CHART

Inches to Millimeters and Centimeters

Inches	MM	CM	Inches	MM	CM
1/8	3	.3	2	51	5.1
1/4	6	.6	3	76	7.6
3/8	10	1.0	4	102	10.2
1/2	13	1.3	5	127	12.7
5/8	16	1.6	6	152	15.2
3/4	19	1.9	7	178	17.8
7/8	22	2.2	8	203	20.3
1	25	2.5	9	229	22.9
1-1/4	32	3.2	10	254	25.4
1-1/2	38	3.8	11	279	27.9
1-3/4	44	4.4	12	305	30.5

Yards to Meters

Yards	Meters	Yards	Meters
1/8	.11	3	2.74
1/4	.23	4	3.66
3/8	.34	5	4.57
1/2	.46	6	5.49
5/8	.57	7	6.40
3/4	.69	8	7.32
7/8	.80	9	8.23
1	.91	10	9.14
2	1.83		

INDEX

INDEX

Continued on next page

INDEX